PENGU

THE PENGU
AN

Rosemary Hemphill was born in Broome, North Western Australia, in 1922. Her early education took place in England where she stayed with her grandparents in Kent. On returning to Australia, she went to St Hilda's, a boarding school in Perth, for the next five years. As Broome was so far away, she visited her home only once a year.

When she left school, Rosemary Hemphill went to a business college in Perth. She met her husband, John, they married when she was nineteen, and he was sent straight to the war. He returned and they decided to move to the freer atmosphere of country life. Mrs Hemphill started growing herbs because she was fascinated by their history and their food value. This hobby created widespread interest and publicity and led to a serious business which her husband is now running. It also led to the publication of her two books *Fragrance and Flavour* and *Spice and Savour*, all of whose recipes were tried out on her two sons. Apart from her herbs, Rosemary Hemphill enjoys writing, painting and cooking.

THE PENGUIN BOOK OF
Herbs and Spices

ROSEMARY HEMPHILL

PENGUIN BOOKS

Penguin Books Ltd, Harmondsworth, Middlesex, England
Penguin Books Australia Ltd, Ringwood, Victoria, Australia
Penguin Books (N.Z.) Ltd, 182–190 Wairau Road, Auckland 10, New Zealand

—

First published as *Fragrance and Flavour* and *Spice and Savour*
by Angus & Robertson, 1959, 1965
First published in this form in Penguin Books 1966
Reprinted 1967, 1968, 1970, 1971, 1972, 1973, 1974, 1975 (twice)

—

Copyright © Rosemary Hemphill, 1959, 1965, 1966

—

Made and printed in Great Britain
by C. Nicholls & Company Ltd
Set in Monotype Garamond

This book is sold subject to the condition
that it shall not, by way of trade or otherwise,
be lent, re-sold, hired out, or otherwise circulated
without the publisher's prior consent in any form of
binding or cover other than that in which it is
published and without a similar condition
including this condition being imposed
on the subsequent purchaser

Contents

Acknowledgements   7

INTRODUCTION

History and Traditions 11	Harvesting 19
The Herb Garden 14	Growing Herbs Indoors 20
Herb Lawns 17	Classification 22
Dried Herbs 18	

HERBS, SPICES AND AROMATIC SEEDS

Allspice	25	Geraniums	83
Angelica	27	Ginger	87
Aniseed	29	Juniper berries	90
Balm	31	Lavender	92
Basil	33	Mace and Nutmeg	95
Bay leaves	37	Marjoram	98
Bergamot	40	Mint	102
Borage	42	Mustard seed	107
Caraway seed	44	Oregano	109
Cardamom seed	46	Paprika	113
Cayenne	48	Parsley	115
Celery seed	50	Pepper	119
Chervil	51	Poppy seed	120
Chicory	54	Rosemary	123
Chilli powder	56	Roses	127
Chives	58	Saffron	131
Cinnamon	60	Sage	134
Cloves	63	Salt	139
Coriander seed	66	Savory	140
Cumin seed	69	Sesame seed	144
Curry powder	71	Tarragon	146
Dill seed	74	Thyme	151
Fennel	78	Turmeric	157
Garlic	81	Vanilla pod	158

Herbal Teas	163
Fragrant Gifts	169
Some Books Consulted	175
Herb Stockists	177
Index	179

ACKNOWLEDGEMENTS

Grateful thanks are expressed to the following people who helped me in one way or another while I was writing this book: Mr and Mrs J. S. Sareen, of the Ministry of External Affairs, New Delhi, for valuable advice on the Indian curry, and for their demonstration of the use of pure silver on the Indian pudding *Kheer*; Mr and Mrs L. M. Chabot, of the Java Restaurant, Dural, for their helpful discussion about Indonesian curries; Mr Douglas Lamb, of the Douglas Lamb Cellars, Sydney, for his useful comments on the most suitable wines to serve with certain food; my mother, for her generous contributions to my herb library, literature which has been invaluable in research for this book; and my husband for his cheerful and unselfish attitude when meals were late and often experimental.

The publishers acknowledge with thanks the permission of the copyright owners to reprint the poem 'The Clove Orange', by Eleanor Farjeon.

FOR JOHN

Introduction

History and Traditions

I know a bank whereon the wild thyme blows,
Where oxlips and the nodding violet grows
Quite over-canopied with luscious woodbine,
With sweet musk-roses, and with eglantine ...

A Midsummer Night's Dream ACT II, SCENE I

It is in the planning and planting of gardens that many people express their sense of the beautiful and find contentment. To some it may be the simple joy of stepping on to a peppermint-scented carpet of pennyroyal in the early morning; to others the pleasure of seeing the jewelled flowers of a favourite tea-tree glistening through the mistiness of a spider's web.

Originally man depended on plants for food and medicine, and many of the ornamental flowers, shrubs and trees that are part of the garden landscape today were once valued for their healing properties as well as for their beauty. All through history there have been stories of gardens – from the splendour of the Hanging Gardens of Babylon, one of the seven wonders of the ancient world, to the monastic 'physic gardens' of medieval days, where monks grew herbs and concocted them into healing potions and salves for the sick.

There is an interesting biblical tale, nearly 2,000 years old, told in *The Bible as History*, of the herbal gardens of the village of Mataria, near Cairo – the Queen of Sheba is said to have taken seeds of balsam as a present to King Solomon, and scented bushes from the seeds grew in Jericho. Many years later Cleopatra took cuttings of these valuable plants to Mataria. Later still, during their flight into Egypt, Joseph, Mary, and Jesus took refuge in these fragrant balsam gardens of Mataria.

A scented garden is not complete without a variety of herbs, and they are very interesting to grow. Each plant has its own characteristic flavour and scent, which may be utilized in cooking, in making fragrant and beneficial 'tisanes' (nourishing

Introduction

decoctions) or gathering and drying for pot-pourri or sweet sachets. Every herb has its own legend too, and it is almost worth growing them for this alone.

Besides their value as flavouring in food, herbs have, of course, traditionally been used in the preparation of medicines. A long time ago man had an affinity with the plant world and a sure, instinctive understanding of it. As Mrs Leyel says in *The Truth About Herbs*, Hippocrates, the 'Father of Medicine', was learned in the preparation of herbs, and of a list left by him of four hundred simples (herbs used medicinally, and medicines made from them), half are still in general use today. As well as balm, basil, fennel, and thyme, Hippocrates' list included less familiar, slightly sinister-sounding herbs like hemlock, henbane, and mandragora, or mandrake, which had the reputation of shrieking when pulled from the ground.

So, whether we grow herbs, eat them, or take them as medicine, they carry us, if we stop to think about them, far back into history. They have been highly important in trade, and wars have been fought over them. In the Middle Ages they were regarded as necessities, not luxuries, for they helped in the preservation of food, as well as being wanted for medicine. They were difficult to obtain, and had to be brought from the Far East first by sea, then by caravan across the desert to be shipped to the great trading ports of Genoa and Venice; then pack animals carried the precious cargo to waiting merchants in northern Europe who finally distributed it. Holland, Spain, France, and Portugal have all struggled at various times to control the spice trade.

When we think of herb gardens established in Europe we may call to mind a rich stew, aromatic with thyme and bay leaves, simmering on the stove in a country kitchen agleam with rows of pots and pans, with geraniums blooming on the window-sill, and a glimpse of a well-stocked herb garden through the shining panes; or, farther back into time, we see a fleeting picture of the garden of some medieval monastery, with its orderly rows of plants cloistered by high walls from the outside world. Beyond that again, herbs and spices take us to hot blue Arabian skies; to hundred-gated Thebes humming

Introduction

with life and trade on the banks of the Nile; to the ancient palace of Knossos on Crete, with its murals of saffron-gatherers; and again to the Queen of Sheba herself, visiting King Solomon at Jerusalem 'with a very great company, and camels that bare spices, and gold in abundance, and precious stones'.

But while we all enjoy the special magic surrounding the legends of herbs and spices, they are valued above all for their practical uses. These have been affirmed in the writings of many civilizations: Egyptian hieroglyphics, the Old Testament, early Greek and Roman documents, Saxon and medieval manuscripts, and the great English herbals of William Turner, John Gerard, and John Parkinson. When reading any history of herbs and spices one is struck by the common sense with which they have been used. Aniseed, for instance, has digestive qualities, and so we read of the Romans finishing their sumptuous feasts with anise cakes. Dill seed has the same attribute, and is often included in old recipes for cooking cabbage, to make this vegetable more digestible. And this combination of romance and practicality continues to the present day. Many national or regional dishes rely on a particular herb or spice for their special character: paprika is the spice which imparts to Hungarian goulash its distinctive flavour and colour; chilli powder gives Chilli con Carne its fire; Spaghetti Bolognese is not complete without oregano; while saffron in Bouillabaisse is traditional.

Some herbs, when dried, are known as spices, but these are simply the dried leaves of culinary plants. True spices are aromatic products from various parts of plants usually indigenous to hot countries, where their flavour is at its best. The part required is collected and dried; it may be the buds, bark, berries, fruit, roots, or – as with saffron – the flower stigmas. Nowadays aromatic culinary seeds are generally grouped with spices under that name, and are gathered when ripe from the spent flower-heads of plants.

The Herb Garden

It is possible for everyone to grow herbs, whether their garden is large or small, or even if they have no garden. People living in flats may grow many herbs successfully in suitable containers; details of how this may be achieved are given in the section Growing Herbs Indoors (page 20).

Although herbs may grow among all the other plants in the garden, it is more satisfactory to have them together – you are not then wondering if the thyme is hiding under the jasmine, or if you will have to disturb the columbines to find the chives! When the herbs are growing together it is an easy matter to survey them at a glance and decide which ones you would like to pick and put in sandwiches,* or in a rice salad, or use in other ways.

Nearly all herbs prefer light, well-drained soil and plenty of sunlight so that they may produce their essential oils. The few that prefer shade and a moist position, such as angelica, bergamot and chervil, may be planted in the shadiest corner, perhaps under a lemon-scented verbena tree, and given the water they require.

A sunny pathway planting of herbs within easy reach of the kitchen has endless possibilities, and a sundial set at a pleasing angle gives interest. A base may be made of stones cemented together, or an old tree stump of the right size is quite effective.

A wheel-garden or a ladder-garden makes compact plant-

---

* Herb sandwiches have a fresh and pleasing flavour – everyone likes them. Spread slices of brown bread – brown seems to go best with herbs – with butter and a little cream cheese or Marmite, fill with chopped herbs and cut off the crusts. Almost any herbs will do, although it is wise to use a little discretion; for instance, marjoram and basil are pungent and go well with chives or parsley. Pennyroyal, which has a strong flavour of peppermint, is best mixed with parsley and a leaf or two of eau-de-Cologne mint; mustard and cress are old favourites; and on very hot days spearmint sandwiches are refreshing.

Introduction

ings. For a wheel-garden, lay an old cartwheel on prepared ground, and plant the herbs between the spokes with either a sundial or a tall, bushy perennial, such as rosemary, wormwood, sage, or lavender, in the middle. Graduate the size of the other herbs as they radiate from the centre, with the low border plants, chives, parsley, pennyroyal and thyme for instance, at the edges. For a ladder-garden, lay the ladder along the ground, and plant herbs between the rungs.

In a larger garden, a corner might be found for a properly enclosed herb garden laid out with geometrical beds. These gardens may vary in size and shape from perhaps a square garden 10 feet by 10 feet to a rectangular garden 18 feet by 25 feet or larger. It is a matter of taste and room. There are various ways of enclosing a garden like this; for a formal effect a low hedge of clipped dwarf box (*Buxus sempervirens*) is traditional, neat and attractive. A scented hedge of either French lavender, hyssop, 'lad's love' (*Artemisia abrotanum*), winter savory or rosemary is equally good. The garden may also be enclosed with crossed saplings for climbing roses to grow over, or a low picket fence, painted white. Brick or stone is used, too, and even though this takes more time to construct it is very attractive when completed.

For those who may wish to attempt a garden of this kind, the following description of a typical one will serve as a guide. An area 25 feet by 18 feet was pegged out and surrounded with a wall, 3 feet high, of 'ballast' stone. The stones were cemented together, not too neatly, so as to give them a rough, weathered look. The wall was made double, with a space in the middle about 12 inches wide to contain soil for plants to grow in. Holes were left in the cement for drainage.

In the middle of the garden there is a sundial, with simple geometrical beds of herbs and stone paths radiating from it. There is also a stone seat, with English lavender growing on either side of it. The same sweet-smelling plant borders the little pathway leading from the herb garden into the rose garden.

With a garden of this type, shrubs and plants of varying heights may be grown from the top of the wall very effectively.

Introduction

Sturdy French lavender, prostrate rosemary, creeping thymes, wormwood, lavender-cotton and the old, scented wallflower are just a few that are suitable.

When planning to grow herbs, have the position and ground ready in time for planting in spring. A sunny aspect and light soil is a good all-round rule for growing herbs. A few such as chervil, bergamot and angelica prefer semi-shade, and this may be arranged by choosing the most protected position for them.

Sow the seeds in seed boxes after the frosts are over, and, when big enough to handle, plant the seedlings out. If well cared for they will grow rapidly and be ready to start using within a few weeks. Water them in dry weather and keep them weeded and cultivated.

Herbs respond to constant picking: chives become sturdier and send out fresh, tender leaves more quickly; parsley and chervil leaves should be picked from the outside always, allowing the new leaves to grow from the middle; basil must have the tops continually picked out to make a sturdy bush and to prevent it from flowering too soon.

The low-growing herbs best suited for edging are pennyroyal, chives, fragrant thyme, chervil, variegated balm, and hyssop. Herbs of medium height are spicy tarragon, coriander, sweet basil, oregano, winter savory, mint, marjoram, lemon balm, and camomile. The taller herbs to use for background planting or to feature as a central point are angelica, lovage, basil, dill, fennel, sage, lavender, rosemary, rue, anchusa, and chicory. Bergamot must be cherished in a sheltered, rather moist position. Mint and tarragon must have room to spread, so it is wise to remember this when planting. Borage is lovely if left to itself and allowed to grow in a misty blue drift in a corner on its own.

The perfumed herbs should be grown for making into scented gifts, or to pick for fragrant posies or 'tussie-mussies' as they were once called. Many of them are used to impart their aroma to certain food. There are the lavenders – English (*Lavandula vera*) and French (*L. dentata* and *L. stoechas*), to name but three varieties. Rosemary is used sparingly in cooking veal and pork dishes, but it is more often grown for its sweet scent and meaning of friendship and remembrance. Rue is the 'herb of grace' and should be near by, for 'where there's rosemary there's rue'. A small amount of the chopped leaves are often used in vegetable cocktails.

Scented-leaved geraniums are also used in flavouring some foods, but are better known for the fragrance of their leaves. Lemon-scented verbena grows into a graceful tree with deliciously perfumed leaves which retain their lemon scent long after they have been dried and are brittle with age; a few fresh leaves impart a delicate flavour to baked milk puddings. Heliotrope or 'cherry pie' is a soft cloud of mauve when in full bloom and is one of the most fragrant herbs; grow it in a sheltered, sunny position.

Wallflowers, the old yellow and tawny ones, contain in the flowers the distilled essence of all the mellow summer scents, warm walls, new-mown hay and the sweetness of all flowers; this plant was once a healing herb. Added to the few which have been mentioned are other well-known plants which were once valuable herbs – roses, violets, jasmine, primroses, clove-pinks, hollyhocks, foxglove and honeysuckle, all of which would be in keeping in a herb garden.

Herb Lawns

Have you ever thought of having a herb lawn, or a pathway made entirely of herbs? Thyme, pennyroyal and camomile are all suitable for this. The hardy *Thymus serpyllum*, if given a chance to establish itself, makes a fragrant carpet. It cannot bear much traffic, so it would have to be grown in a special corner of its own. Thyme, grown over a mound of earth, makes a soft and scented seat; plant established roots, lift apart in the early spring and keep weed-free and well watered.

Pennyroyal spreads very quickly, is extremely hardy, and discourages weeds once it has formed a thick mat. The fresh peppermint scent is released when it is trodden on, and it would be a pity to mow it in the spring when its small spires of

Introduction

lavender-coloured flowers are in bloom. Plant roots two to three feet apart in the spring and autumn.

English camomile (*Anthemis nobilis*) is the only one of the three which needs mowing. E. S. Rohde says: 'I wonder how many of the people who attend the royal garden parties at Buckingham Palace realize that big stretches of one of the lawns are planted with camomile?' It makes an excellent lawn and is particularly hardy in hot, dry weather, remaining green and fresh-looking. It may be walked on as much as an ordinary grass lawn. Put in the plants 4 inches apart in spring or autumn, roll it and weed and water it. Paths of these carpeting herbs may replace stone or brick paths in the herb garden.

Dried Herbs

As the season advances and the herbs approach maturity it is time to decide which to dry for winter use. Although leaves of marjoram, thyme and oregano are always available, they are even more pungent when dried, and now is the time, while the atmosphere is dry, to do it. Herbs should be harvested just before the buds open into full flower for the greatest flavour and abundance of natural oils.

Gather them in dry weather, after the dew has left them and before the hot sun has drawn out the natural oils, hang them up to dry in bundles in an airy passageway, or lay them on paper in a dark cupboard. Oven-drying is not good unless wet weather makes it necessary, as much of the flavour is lost in this way. The drying time varies from about twelve days to three weeks. When dry, strip the leaves from the stalks on to clean paper and pour them into clean, dry, airtight jars which have been clearly labelled. Keep the herbs separate so that blending becomes a personal choice. It is interesting to experiment with flavours.

When dried herbs are used, a much smaller quantity is needed for flavouring than of herbs picked straight from the garden, for the flavour is more highly concentrated

Introduction

in the dried product. If fresh herbs are called for in a recipe and you do not have them, a fairly general rule to follow is to use one third of the amount of dried herbs. Usually herbs and spices are meant to complement and bring out the flavour of the dish in which they are being used, not to dominate it, although there are occasions when a greater quantity is called for. I remember eating a friend's delicious apple pie – an old family recipe – with a wonderful pastry dusky with allspice and cinnamon. A tablespoon of allspice and a dessertspoon of cinnamon* are sifted with two cups of self-raising flour and a pinch of salt, then stirred with a packed cup of brown sugar, the whole rubbed together with four ounces of butter and moistened with one well-beaten egg. (I was told to use a little milk if the mixture was not moist enough.) The pastry should be rolled out thinly, and divided into two pieces for lining a greased dish and for covering the sugared, lemon-flavoured apples.

Harvesting

With the coming of autumn in the herb garden, the flowers which have been left to bear next season's crop of herbs must be gathered when the seeds are ripe. Put the seeds away in labelled airtight envelopes or little jars. Cut out dead stalks in the garden and trim the plants.

When winter comes sweet basil will be missed, but instead there are fresh marjoram leaves, which are very aromatic and pungent and seem to suit the season; winter vegetables after all have stronger flavours.

By mid-winter the herb garden will be lying dormant, waiting for spring, and as many of the herbs are perennials, their second year will be worth seeing. It is a good idea at this time to give the ground a light top-dressing of well-decayed poultry humus.

When spring comes again and the garden is established, it is

* Level measures should be used in all the recipes in this book unless otherwise stated.

Introduction

time to think of the other aspects connected with herb gardening. The sweet-smelling herbs, flowers and fruit needed for making pot-pourri, lavender bags, sachets, pomander oranges, herb pillows, scented coat-hangers and perfumed rubbing lotions are ready. These make delightful and unusual gifts at Christmas; some ideas are given on pages 167–173.

Growing Herbs Indoors

People who live in flats and would like to grow herbs may do so successfully if a few simple rules are followed. First of all the right soil mixture is important, and it should consist of sand, leaf-mould and soil in equal parts. Nurseries sometimes sell this mixture in polythene bags. Secondly, herbs love sunlight so at some stage during the day it is desirable for them to bask in it, particularly by an open window. The third point to remember is to keep them watered – once a day should be sufficient. About once a fortnight add a little liquid fertilizer, which is obtainable at most nurseries, to the watering can.

When planting, cover the hole in the container with a few pieces of broken crock or some stones, and then fill with soil. Put in the seedlings, firming them well with the hands, and water well.

Nearly all herbs will grow in containers, the taller-growing varieties such as Florence fennel, borage and sage becoming satisfactorily dwarfed with the confined root-space. The herbs of low and medium growth, sweet basil, chervil, chives, marjoram, parsley, and thyme, are all excellent for this purpose. Herbs with rampant root systems, for instance balm, winter savory, the mints, oregano, pennyroyal and tarragon, should be put severely on their own, or they will choke out the others. Lavender, rosemary, and the scented-leaved geraniums will not attain the height they would reach if growing in the garden, but if re-potted every year with new soil, and when necessary given a larger container, they will give pleasure for

Introduction

a very long time. Angelica, chicory and lovage grow too high to be considered.

There are various containers on the market suitable for growing herbs in, and, starting from the kitchen, here are a few suggestions: pots of terra-cotta or china grouped on kitchen window ledges are excellent and may be moved about for convenience; let the mint run riot in a squat six-inch azalea pot; a trough of tin, cement or terra-cotta on the window-sill, with several herbs grouped together, is convenient, a good combination being marjoram, chives and parsley, although this is really a matter of personal choice. A graceful, black wrought-iron stand on inch-high legs filled with herbs in china pots, or a trough fitted snugly into it, may be used either on a kitchen window-sill or as a centrepiece on the dining-room table; the leaves may be snipped off to flavour a French salad being mixed at the table.

For balconies, roof gardens, back doors or where space is otherwise restricted, a large 'strawberry pot' with from six to nine pockets is a good idea. The procedure for filling this container is to prepare the soil and put in the plants as the pot is filled with earth, leaving the most decorative herb until last for the top. The soil may be bought ready mixed, or it may be prepared by mixing equal quantities of sand, leaf-mould and soil. With this light soil, water reaches every herb, right down to the bottom. Experiments have shown that a heavier soil combination is a failure. The sand is necessary to prevent the soil from clogging, and the leaf-mould is important for airiness and fertilizing, and as mentioned earlier, this mixture is excellent for other types of containers also.

Let imagination help you in deciding the containers and stands to use. Secondhand or antique shops are a treasure-trove to discerning eyes. With a little paint or polish the most unlikely article may turn out to be an original and striking holder.

Classification

It is interesting to know that some herbs differing widely in appearance and flavour belong to the same family. For instance, mint, thyme, basil, and rosemary are all members of the large family Labiatae, recognized by their square stems and two-lipped flowers. And tarragon, one of the most popular culinary herbs, belongs to a family (Compositae) which numbers among its members such plants as chrysanthemums, lettuce, the common daisy, and asters: these plants have composite flower-heads made up of tightly clustered florets, hence the botanical name given to the family.

For easy classification and to show their natural grouping, the herbs, spices, and aromatic seeds popular in cooking are grouped below:

Herbs

angelica	chervil	parsley
balm	chives	rosemary
basil	garlic	sage
bay leaves	marjoram	savory
bergamot	mint	tarragon
borage	oregano	thyme

Spices

allspice	cloves	paprika
cayenne	ginger	pepper
chilli powder	mace	saffron
cinnamon	nutmeg	turmeric

Aromatic Seeds

aniseed	cumin seed	poppy seed
caraway seed	dill seed	sesame seed
cardamom seed	fennel seed	vanilla pod
celery seed	juniper berries	
coriander seed	mustard seed	

*Herbs, Spices and
Aromatic Seeds*

Allspice

Allspice (*Pimenta officinalis*) comes from a tropical tree that is native to America and is also cultivated in the West Indies and Jamaica. The small sun-dried berries are sometimes known as pimento or Jamaica pepper, but are usually called allspice because the aroma and taste seem to be a combination of cinnamon, cloves, and nutmeg. Allspice is not a mixture of these three spices, as is sometimes thought.

Ground allspice is used in many spice blends and as a flavouring for various cakes, soups, meat dishes, milk puddings and vegetables. The berries are often tied in a muslin bag for use in the making of preserves, pickles, and chutney. Ground allspice with cinnamon helps to give pot-pourri its spicy fragrance.

SPICED VEAL ROLL

1 shoulder of veal, boned
3 oz. soft breadcrumbs
1 dessertspoon seeded raisins
grated rind of an orange
2 teaspoons mixed herbs
a few pieces of butter
1 dessertspoon chopped shallot or onion
salt and pepper
4 tablespoons butter or margarine
1 teaspoon ground allspice
orange juice

Mix together the breadcrumbs, raisins, orange rind, herbs, pieces of butter, and shallot. Season with salt and pepper. Roll the meat up with this stuffing in the centre, tie with string, and rub the surface with butter and 1 teaspoon ground allspice. Put in a baking dish with 4 tablespoons fat (butter or margarine) and the juice from the grated orange. Bake in a moderate oven (gas 4, electric 350–75 °F.), basting frequently. (If the liquid is reducing too much, add a little stock or water.) Allow 25 minutes to the lb. and 25 minutes over. If the liquid is too thin it may be thickened with a little flour and poured over the veal, or served separately in a gravy boat.

Allspice

FRIED ORANGE SLICES

Cut the pithy ends from oranges and discard. Slice the fruit into thin rounds and cover both sides with a mixture of sugar and ground allspice. Melt some butter or margarine and gently fry the orange slices in it, turning until the rinds are lightly browned. Serve hot with roast duck, rabbit, veal, or pork.

ROSE CREAMS

Delicious with black coffee after dinner, this exquisite and rather exotic fondant brings a little of the Golden Road to Samarkand into the recipe collection: '... I will make her sweets like flowers. I will perfume my sweets with the perfume of roses, so that she shall say "a rose!" and smell before she tastes ...' (*Hassan*, by James Elroy Flecker).

½ lb. icing sugar	a few drops of rose water
1 teaspoon ground allspice	(obtainable from the chemist)
1 egg-white	red food colouring

Sift the icing sugar with the allspice. Beat the egg-white slightly, and gradually add half the spiced icing sugar, beating well, then the rose water and enough colouring to make a rosy pink. Add the rest of the icing sugar, to make a stiff consistency. Roll the fondant out on a flat board that has been sprinkled with icing sugar. Cut into rounds with a small cutter and leave to harden.

ROSE-GERANIUM JELLY

This is a special preserve in the same mood as Rose Creams: delicately scented, ruby coloured, and glistening, it may be put on the table with roast baby lamb, veal or poultry, or spread on thin slices of bread and butter.

1 small bunch of rose-geranium leaves (about ½ pint)	juice of 2 small lemons or 1 large lemon
5 cups sugar	4 cups water
1 teaspoon whole allspice	4 oz. powdered pectin
	red food colouring

Wash the rose-geranium leaves and steep them in the sugar, allspice and lemon juice for 1 hour. Place in a saucepan with

Angelica

the water and bring to the boil. Strain, add the pectin, and boil again, stirring for about a minute. Add the food colouring. Pour into small clean jars, with a rose-geranium leaf in each one. Seal the jars.

Angelica

As its name suggests, the perennial herb angelica (*Angelica archangelica*) has heavenly associations in ancient folklore. In *Herbs and Herb Gardening* E. S. Rohde says that, according to tradition, an angel revealed its qualities in a dream during a time of plague, and a piece of the root held in the mouth was commended to drive away the 'pestilentiall aire'.

It was very highly regarded in the old herb gardens, every part of the plant having some particular use. Today, oil distilled from the seeds and roots is used in flavouring liqueurs and wines, and the leaves are used in making beneficial tisanes, and for flavouring stewed fruit. Candied angelica, for which the stalk and leaf stems are used, is well known.

Angelica grows up to six feet in height, and unlike most herbs prefers a moist, rich soil and shade. The seed will not germinate unless it is very fresh.

CANDIED ANGELICA

It is well worth while candying your own angelica; it is not much trouble, but takes a little time. If you plan ahead and quick results are not expected, then you are half way to having it done.

Select young stems and stalks of angelica. Cut into 4 or 5 inch lengths and place in a glass or crockery vessel, pour over them a boiling solution of 1 pint water and $\frac{1}{4}$ lb. salt. Cover and leave for 24 hours. Lift out, drain on a wire drainer, peel and wash in cold water.

Make a syrup of $1\frac{1}{2}$ lb. sugar and $1\frac{1}{2}$ pints water, and boil for 10 minutes. Place the angelica in the boiling syrup for 20 minutes; lift out and drain for 4 days on a wire drainer.

Angelica

Boil again for 20 minutes in the same syrup. Allow to cool in the syrup, lift out and drain for 3 or 4 days. Strew well with sugar and store in airtight jars.

Trifles and cakes are decorated with candied angelica cut into leaves, stems and fancy shapes, and the Italian sweet cassata has angelica in it.

STEWED RHUBARB AND ANGELICA LEAVES

1 *bunch rhubarb*	4 *young angelica leaves*
½ *pint water*	2 *thin curls of lemon peel*
4 *oz. sugar*	

Cut up the rhubarb and put it in a saucepan with the water, sugar, lemon peel and angelica leaves. Bring to the boil, and simmer until tender.

Serve chilled with whipped cream or yoghurt.

GLAZED PEARS

4 *large pears*	*angelica*
1 *cup red or black currant purée or passion-fruit pulp*	1 *teaspoon cinnamon or* 4 *coriander seeds*
1 *cup water*	*a little butter*
½ *cup sugar*	

Wash and core the pears, which should be quite dry, from the stalk end. In each hollow put a knob of butter, a little sugar, and a little cinnamon or 1 coriander seed. Place in a saucepan and pour over them a syrup made from the sugar and water boiled together for 10 minutes. Cover and simmer slowly until just tender, ladling the syrup over continually. Add the purée.

Lift the pears out carefully and put on a dish. Pour the purée and syrup over the pears. Decorate each pear with a stalk of angelica. Chill, and serve with heavy cream.

Instructions for making angelica tea are given on page 166.

Aniseed

Anise (*Pimpinella anisum*, one of the Umbelliferae) is a sun-loving annual plant, native to Middle Eastern countries. The clusters of white flowers are followed by small oval seeds which are light brown in colour and taste warmly of licorice. Anise was known many thousands of years ago: it is referred to in the Bible and, as I mentioned in the Introduction, the Romans ate cakes made with these digestion-aiding seeds to conclude their enormous feasts. Helen Noyes Webster quotes from Grieve and Leyel: 'It was used in a spiced cake at the end of a meal by the Romans in Virgil's time to prevent indigestion; a cake which was brought in at the end of a marriage feast, it is perhaps the origin of today's spicy wedding cake.'

Anise is used extensively in cooking, in medicine for digestive complaints, and as an ingredient in the liqueur Anisette. It is grown mainly for the seeds, although the leaves may be used in salads and as a garnish. Aniseed flavours breads, rolls, cakes, biscuits, and sweet pastry for fruit pies and tarts. It may also be used in cheeses, in milk beverages and puddings, and when cooking vegetables such as carrots and cabbage, when little or no water is used.

With some of the other fragrant seeds, aniseed may be pressed into butter to be spread on top of 'brown-and-serve' rolls before they are put into the oven. Line a basket with a table napkin and fill it with hot rolls, some topped with aniseed, others with sesame seed, poppy seed, dill seed, celery seed, or caraway seed. If you have herbs growing, garnish with leaves of anise, burnet or dill. These rolls are excellent to serve with a main dish for luncheon or supper, the seeds giving them a delicious flavour and crunchiness.

RED CABBAGE CASSEROLE WITH PORK SAUSAGES

Aniseed gives its quota to the other delicious smells which help to make this a fragrant winter dish for six hungry people.

Aniseed

Serve it at supper-time with baked jacket potatoes, and with mulled ale (see recipe opposite).

1 red cabbage	¼ pint strong chicken stock
3 onions, peeled and chopped	(made with 1 cube)
3 green apples, chopped with the skin on	1 teaspoon black peppercorns
	½ teaspoon salt
3 tablespoons demerara sugar	1 dessertspoon aniseed
2 tablespoons cider vinegar	2 lb pork sausages
	½ lb. bacon

Shred the cabbage and put it into a large casserole with the onion, apple, sugar, vinegar, chicken stock, peppercorns, salt and aniseed. Mix well, put the lid on, and bake in a slow oven (gas 1, electric 300°F.) for 3 hours, putting scrubbed potatoes into the oven for the last 1½ hours. Towards the end of the cooking time, fry the sausages and bacon, turning them until browned and cooked. Put them into the cabbage mixture before serving with the baked potatoes.

ANISEED CARROTS

Cut carrots into straws, put them in a saucepan with 2 tablespoons water, 1 tablespoon demerara sugar, 1 oz. butter, and 1 teaspoon aniseed, adding some salt and pepper. Put the lid on and simmer gently for 10 to 15 minutes, when they will be cooked yet crisp and slightly candied.

ANISE COOKIES

4 oz. butter or margarine	a pinch of salt
6 oz. demerara sugar	1 cup rolled oats
1 egg	1½ cups desiccated coconut
4 oz. self-raising flour	2 teaspoons aniseed

Cream the butter and sugar, add the egg and beat well. Stir in the sifted flour and salt, and add the rolled oats, coconut, and aniseed, mixing well together to a stiff consistency. Roll into small balls between the hands, put on a greased oven tray, and bake in a moderate oven (gas 4, electric 350–75°F.) for 12 to 15 minutes. Cool on the tray before storing.

MULLED ALE

This recipe is from *Mrs Beeton's Book of Household Management*.

1 quart good ale
1 glass rum or brandy
1 tablespoon castor sugar
a pinch of ground cloves
a pinch of grated nutmeg
a good pinch of ground ginger

Put the ale, sugar, cloves, nutmeg and ginger into an ale warmer or stewpan, and bring nearly to boiling point. Add the brandy, and more sugar and flavouring if necessary, and serve at once.

Balm

Balm (*Melissa officinalis*) is an easy perennial plant to grow. Like the mint family it prefers part shade and a moist position, and in the autumn it should be cut down to the ground. It has quite a rampant root system, but is easy to keep in check.

In spring the young lemon-scented leaves are fresh and attractive, and it grows rapidly into a thick and bushy plant about two and a half feet high. In summer the series of small, white flowers carried on long stems are a great attraction to bees.

Balm was indispensable in the old herb garden. Refreshing teas and healing ointments were made from the leaves, and bee hives were often rubbed with it. The leaves are a valuable ingredient in pot-pourri too, the rather piercing lemon scent complementing some of the sweeter flower scents. A pot-pourri should be like well-cooked food that has many ingredients in its composition, the whole being a pleasing blend, but no one flavour or aroma being too predominant.

Balm, or lemon balm as it is often called, dries well and retains its scent. A few dried leaves put in the teapot with your usual Indian tea makes an invigorating drink for fatigue, and in hot weather is refreshing.

Variegated balm (*M. officinalis variegata*) is grown more for its appearance than for practical purposes, although a leaf

Balm

floated on top of an iced drink looks attractive. It is a perennial, of spreading habit, growing no more than twelve inches high, and is most effective with its green and pale-gold foliage for rockeries and borders, and in flower arrangements too. It is very aromatic, the whole plant smelling of lemons. It must be watered in dry weather, and protected from too much frost.

The following recipes are for lemon balm, as it is hardier, but a few leaves of the variegated type are suitable for garnishing.

BALM AND MARSHMALLOW CUSTARD

1 pint milk
2 eggs
1½ tablespoons sugar
6 marshmallows
1 tablespoon fresh balm leaves, or 1 dessertspoon dried and crumbled balm leaves
1 vanilla pod

Put the marshmallows in the bottom of a well-buttered fireproof dish. Whisk the eggs and sugar together, add the milk, beat well and pour over the marshmallows. Put in the vanilla, and sprinkle the balm on top. Place the dish in a shallow pan of cold water and bake slowly in a medium oven until set.

Serve chilled with cream – it seems to go particularly well with slices of fresh sugared pineapple.

BALM AND ORANGE FROSTED
(A refreshing summer drink)

1 pint orange juice
½ pint lemon juice
1 pint water
2 bottles ginger ale
1 bunch balm leaves
4 oz. sugar
ice cubes

Mix juices, balm leaves, sugar and water, and chill overnight. Strain, add ginger ale just before serving, and pour into glasses over cubes of ice. Float a balm leaf on the top of each drink.

BALM DRESSING WITH ORANGE SALAD

This salad is excellent with roast duck. It may also be served with turkey or ham.

Peel 4 large oranges, cut in sections and lay in a dish with thinly sliced green peppers. Make a French dressing (1 tablespoon herb vinegar to 3 tablespoons oil) and stir in 1 tablespoon of finely chopped balm. Pour over the oranges and allow to marinate for a few hours before serving.

Basil

Once having used basil in cooking you will think of the two as synonymous, although the story of 'Isabella and the Pot of Basil', immortalized in John Keats's poem, is probably more often associated with its name. Do not let that rather grisly tale turn you aside from this truly wonderful herb, for the whole plant has a unique mouth-watering aroma which is released at the merest touch and makes you want to pick it at once and use it in all sorts of ways. It came originally from India, where as *tulasi* it was used in many religious and superstitious rites. Other countries adopted it centuries ago, and it figures prominently in Greek, Italian and French cooking.

Basil belongs to the Labiatae family, and there are over forty types, each differing from the others in some way – in the height reached by the plant or perhaps in the size or shape, sometimes even the colour, of the leaves.

The two varieties that are the most useful and easy to grow are sweet basil (*Ocimum basilicum*) and bush basil (*O. minimum*). They are both annuals, bush basil growing to a height of only six inches or so. If sown in a warm, sunny position in light, rich soil after the frosts, sweet basil will grow to a height of two feet until frosty weather comes again. Because of the size of its leaves and rich perfume, sweet basil is the most popular one for drying.

Once the plant is established, keep nipping off the tops, a process that will make it branch out and spread into a sturdy bush. The nipped tops should not be thrown away but used. Once you have let the plant flower, which it tries to do very early and is one of the reasons for nipping, it can be cut right down, and the branches hung up to dry for winter use.

Although this herb is more pungent when fresh, it retains

its flavour well when dried. When thoroughly dry, rub the leaves and flowers off the stalks on to paper and pour into clean, dry, airtight jars.

Basil is known best for its affiliation with tomatoes. It is delicious when chopped and sprinkled on circles of ice-cold, red tomatoes, on baked tomatoes, in tomato purée and in tomato juice. There are endless ways of using it with tomatoes. It is not, however, limited to being used with this vegetable. It combines well with eggs, in potato salad, mixes well in a cold rice salad, and imparts its flavour when added to soups and stews.

Cold rice salad, laced generously with chopped green herbs with basil predominating, is excellent. Boil the rice in the usual way and empty it into a colander, run cold water over it to separate the grains, drain, and mix well with the French dressing given below. There are endless varieties of ingredients to put with it from prawns, olives, nuts, grated onion and diced celery to chopped ham or bacon, asparagus tips, tomatoes and cucumber cut into chunks, and slivers of cheese. Pick sprays of fresh basil from the garden, remove the leaves and chop them very finely and put them into the bowl before adding the dressing. Toss the salad well before serving.

Basil makes a savoury vinegar. It is simply made by packing the fresh leaves into a jar and pouring 1 pint of wine vinegar over them. Cover tightly and allow to infuse on a sunny shelf for two weeks. Strain and use in French dressing.

FRENCH DRESSING

1 tablespoon wine or herb vinegar
3 tablespoons olive or groundnut oil
salt, pepper and a pinch of sugar

Mix these ingredients together in a small basin or cup, and toss a salad with it immediately before serving.

BAKED TOMATOES AND BASIL

1 lb. tomatoes
2 onions
1 tablespoon chopped basil

breadcrumbs
butter, sugar, salt and pepper

Basil

Slice the tomatoes and onions. Put a layer of tomatoes in the bottom of a buttered pie-dish, then a dessertspoon of basil and a layer of onions. Season with salt and pepper, a sprinkling of sugar and dot lightly with butter. Repeat this until the dish is full, then top quite thickly with breadcrumbs and pieces of butter. Bake in a moderate oven (gas 4, electric 350°F.) for 20 minutes. The tempting aroma that greets you when this is taken from the oven is delicious. Serve it hot with roast beef or lamb.

BASIL AND TOMATO ASPIC

A smooth-textured and delicately flavoured aspic. Prepare it a day or so beforehand and keep it chilled in the refrigerator, unmoulding just before serving. Accompany with thin slices of ham, a tossed green salad, and hot rolls.

- 2 pints tomato juice
- 1 cup mayonnaise
- 3 envelopes, or 3 rounded dessertspoons, gelatine
- ½ cup chopped shallots
- 3 tablespoons demerara sugar
- 2 dessertspoons basil
- 2 tablespoons lemon juice
- 1 cup diced celery
- 1 green capsium, chopped
- 1 small jar stuffed olives, sliced
- salt and pepper

Soften the gelatine in 1½ cups of the tomato juice. Put the remainder of the juice into a saucepan with the shallots, basil, sugar and lemon juice. Season with salt and pepper. Bring to the boil, and simmer for a few minutes. Remove from the stove and stir in the dissolved gelatine, then the mayonnaise, celery, capsicum and olives. Put in a cool place, and when beginning to set pour into a rinsed-out mould. Chill in the refrigerator. Serves 8.

LAMB'S LIVER WITH BASIL

As basil and lamb's liver go well together, the following recipe is a particularly good one.

- 1 lamb's liver
- flour, seasoned with salt and pepper
- 2 tablespoons chopped basil
- ½ lb. bacon
- butter or margarine

Fry the bacon and put on a dish in a warm place. Melt the fat, and gently cook the liver which has been cut up and rolled in the flour. At the last add the basil and 1 cup of stock and a little wine if liked. Arrange the liver with the bacon, and pour the gravy from the pan over. Serve hot.

DOLMAS

An unusual way of serving liver with a green vegetable, both aromatically spiced with basil, is shown in this recipe for stuffed leaves of cabbage, spinach, or vine leaves.

cabbage, spinach, or vine leaves	1 cup cooked rice
1 lb. lamb's liver	3 or 4 teaspoons basil
2 oz. butter or margarine	several rashers of fat bacon
2 cloves of garlic, finely chopped	2 tablespoons red or white wine,
1 red or green capsicum, chopped	stock, or water
1 onion, chopped	salt and pepper

Allow 3 or 4 cabbage, spinach, or vine leaves for each person. Wash the leaves selected for stuffing, cut out any hard stalk, blanch in boiling water for a few minutes, and drain. Soak the liver in salted water, remove the skin, and chop the meat into small pieces. Melt the butter in a saucepan then soften the onion, garlic, and capsicum in it. Add the meat and allow it to cook gently, turning frequently. Stir in the rice and basil, and season with salt and pepper.

Spread out the blanched leaves, put mounds of meat and rice mixture on each one, and roll up into parcels. Place in layers in a casserole with pieces of bacon between the layers and on top. Pour in the liquid and put the casserole lid on. Bake in a slow oven (gas $\frac{1}{2}$, electric 250°F.) for $1\frac{1}{2}$ to 2 hours. If during the cooking it becomes a little dry, add more liquid.

FISH ROE ENTRÉE

$\frac{1}{2}$ lb. soft roes	breadcrumbs
plain flour	butter
3 teaspoons basil	salt and pepper
$\frac{1}{4}$ pint cream	

Roll the roes in seasoned plain flour and lay them in a buttered ovenproof dish. Sprinkle with the basil, add the cream, top with breadcrumbs, and dot with butter. Bake in a moderate oven (gas 4, electric 350°F.) for 10 to 15 minutes. Serve hot.

Bay Leaves

Leaves from the Bay Tree (*Laurus nobilis*, one of the Lauraceae family) are almost an everyday ingredient in cooking, but there is hardly any mention of the tree in gardening books or catalogues. They are not easy to obtain, and yet, quite apart from its aromatic and useful leaves, the bay grows into a most attractive tree. It is native to Mediterranean areas, and its leaves were once made into wreaths to crown the heroes of ancient Greece and Rome. An oil used in herbal medicine is extracted from the leaves and berries.

Doctor William Turner, a sixteenth-century physician, observes that 'when they are casten into the fyre they crake wonderfully'. And Nicholas Culpeper in the seventeenth century wrote that 'neither witch nor devil, thunder nor lightning, will hurt a man where a bay tree is'.

Although a bay tree will grow to grand proportions, it may be cut back periodically without any adverse effect. It makes an attractive standard tree if you encourage it to grow on one central stem by snipping off any laterals or suckers, rounding the top into a large glossy green ball; the formal shape of the leaves gives bay trees cultivated in this way an extremely elegant appearance. They are sometimes seen growing in tubs at the entrance doors of restaurants and hotels, and in the miniature gardens of penthouses.

Look after your bay tree; it is a cheerful sight when healthy, but depressing when neglected. When grown in a tub it is most ornamental. Do not let it dry out, and top-dress occasionally with well-decayed manure or bone dust.

Bay leaves may be used straight from the tree, or dried. This is simply done by leaving them in a cool, airy place for a few days and then putting them in an airtight jar.

A bay leaf is used in a bouquet of herbs, or *bouquet garni*, the other herbs being usually a sprig each of thyme, marjoram and parsley. These should be tied together, and are often

Bay Leaves

removed before the dish in which they have been cooking is served.

It is a good idea to include a bay leaf in soups, stews, and casseroles, in the making of stock, and when cooking corned beef, salted mutton, pickled pork, tongue, poultry and fish. Bay leaves are used, also, in the making of pot-pourri, and our grandmothers often used them to flavour milk puddings.

WELSH STEW

My mother's recipe for Welsh stew, given to her by her mother, is succulent with meat and gravy, and fragrant with thyme and bay leaves. The stock may be made with beef cubes.

2 lb. beef	2 bay leaves
1½ pints beef stock	thyme
a bunch of leeks	salt and pepper
1 turnip	a lump of sugar

Cut the beef into neat pieces and put in a casserole with the stock. Bring to the boil, then simmer for ¾ hour. Add the white part of the leeks, well washed and cut up, the turnip cut into dice, 2 bay leaves, a spray of thyme, season with salt and pepper, and add a lump of sugar. Stew gently for about 1 hour. Serve in the casserole.

STEAK CASSEROLE WITH BAY LEAVES AND PICKLED WALNUTS

1 lb. steak	1 glass red wine or stock
4 pickled walnuts	1 finely sliced onion
2 bay leaves	1 finely sliced tomato
2 tablespoons flour	salt, pepper and sugar

Cut the steak into pieces and roll well in the flour. Put in layers in a casserole dish the steak, bay leaves, onion, tomato, pickled walnuts, salt, pepper and sugar to taste. (Used sparingly, sugar helps to bring out the flavour in food.) Lastly, sprinkle any left-over flour into the casserole and pour over the wine or stock. Cover and cook in a medium oven for 2 hours.

STUFFED CABBAGE LEAVES

The following recipe for stuffed cabbage leaves is sufficient for four people, allowing two rolls for each person. The bay leaves wonderfully impart their individual aromatic flavour to the cabbage.

1 *cabbage*	2 *or* 3 *bay leaves*
1 *lb. minced steak*	1 *small teaspoon crushed coriander*
1 *chopped onion*	*seeds*
¾ *cup cooked rice*	*salt and pepper, parsley*
1 *breakfast cup stock*	*cornflour*

Cut the leaves carefully from the cabbage and select the most suitable for rolling the meat mixture in. Trim, put in boiling water and cook for 7 minutes. Drain in a colander.

Fry the onion in a little fat until soft, and put in a bowl with the minced steak and rice. Season with salt and pepper, add the coriander seeds and mix well. Put a good tablespoon of this mixture on to each cabbage leaf, roll up neatly and place the rolls in a casserole dish with the bay leaves. Pour in the stock, cover and simmer gently in the oven for 45 minutes. Lift out the stuffed cabbage leaves carefully, arrange on a dish, and keep hot while the stock is thickened on the stove with a little blended cornflour.

Pour the liquid over the cabbage rolls and sprinkle them with finely chopped parsley. Serve with thick slices of crusty French bread.

FISH SPECIAL

Another excellent dish from my mother's recipe book.

Roll fillets of fish prettily and place them in a buttered fireproof dish with 1 or 2 bay leaves. Over the fillets pour a glass of white wine and then sprinkle them with a layer of chopped chives or shallots. Add a few more pieces of butter and cook in a closed dish long and slowly. If allowed to get cold, the fish will be surrounded by a rich jelly.

RICE AND TREACLE PUDDING

Here is a plain but nourishing milk pudding from the family recipe book. It is popular with children.

In an ovenproof dish blend together 2 scant tablespoons

rice and 1 tablespoon golden syrup. Gradually incorporate 1 pint milk. Dot with butter, and lay a bay leaf on top. Bake in a slow oven (gas ½, electric 275 °F.) for about 1½ hours. May be eaten hot or cold, with cream.

Bergamot

Bergamot (*Monarda didyma*) is a perennial and is one of the most scented of all herbs. The leaves and the flowers have a delicious fragrance which bees love, and it is sometimes known as bee balm.

This herb originated in North America, and received its botanical name from Nicholas Monardes, a Spanish physician who discovered it in the sixteenth century.

There are several varieties of *Monarda*, all popular in herbaceous borders, and bearing pale blue, pink, mauve or scarlet flowers. It is the latter, Cambridge Scarlet, which is the most popular. It grows to four feet in the right position, and being similar to the mint family it is happiest in a shady, rather moist position.

After flowering it dies right down and should be cut to the ground, when new leaves soon appear. The clump must be watered well in dry weather or it will die right out.

With the coming of spring and warmer weather the flower stalks rapidly begin to grow taller every day. At this time a dressing of well-decayed poultry manure helps growth, and in early summer the wonderful heads of scarlet pom-poms begin to bloom. These are full of honey, and are edible. A tossed green salad with shredded bergamot flowers added at the last not only looks attractive but tastes excellent too. The flavour is not cloying or sweet, but delicately pungent.

The young leaves may be added to a salad, and they impart an elusive flavour to cooking. They combine particularly well with pork, having something of the pungency of sage, and yet the scent of rosemary as well.

It is interesting to know that oil of bergamot does not come from this plant, but from a citrus tree, the bergamot orange (*Citrus bergamia*). The flavour is similar, which is the reason for this herb's everyday name.

PORK SAUSAGES WITH APPLE AND BERGAMOT

- 1½ *lb. good pork sausages*
- 2 *large cooking apples, sliced*
- 1 *oz. butter or margarine*
- ½ *pint water or stock*
- 1 *sliced onion*
- 2 *cloves garlic*
- 1 *tablespoon chopped bergamot leaves*
- *flour, cinnamon, salt and pepper*

Fry the apple (the peel may be left on for added flavour), onion and garlic in the fat until soft, and remove from the pan. Roll the sausages in flour and fry until brown.

Place in alternate layers in a casserole dish the apple, onion and garlic mixture, the sausages, bergamot leaves, salt, pepper and a light dusting of cinnamon. Pour over the stock or water, cover, and simmer for 1½ hours.

BERGAMOT SALAD AS AN ACCOMPANIMENT TO BRAWN

- 1 *large or medium lettuce*
- 1 *dessertspoon young bergamot leaves*
- 1 *clove of garlic*
- 3 *bergamot flower heads*
- 4 *hard-boiled eggs*
- *French dressing*

Wash the lettuce and dry it thoroughly. It is a good idea to do this some hours before you need the lettuce, and then put it in a covered dish in the refrigerator, so that it is cool and crisp when wanted.

Wash the young bergamot leaves, which may be left whole, but if possible do not wash the flowers as some of the scent is then lost.

Rub a wooden bowl with a clove of garlic, put in the torn-up lettuce leaves, bergamot leaves and sliced hard-boiled eggs. Add the French dressing (1 tablespoon herb vinegar to 3 tablespoons olive or groundnut oil, salt, pepper, and a little sugar), and toss well. At the last tear the heads of the bergamot flowers into the salad, toss again and serve.

Borage

BERGAMOT SAUCE

1 *tablespoon chopped shallots*	1 *dessertspoon flour*
1 *oz. butter or margarine*	1 *dessertspoon chopped bergamot*
1 *wineglass white wine*	*leaves*
juice of ½ lemon	*salt and pepper*

Melt the fat and fry the shallots until soft, add the flour and stir until blended, then slowly add the wine and lemon juice. When thickened stir in the bergamot leaves, salt and pepper, and cook for a little longer. Serve hot. This is delicious with roast pork.

OSWEGO TEA

A famous refreshing tea is made from bergamot leaves in Oswego, in America, known as Oswego tea. During hot weather a few leaves of the herb, either fresh or dried, may be added to an infusion of ordinary tea.

Borage

Borage (*Borago officinalis*) was once more highly esteemed than it is now. It was firmly believed that a conserve of the flowers drove away melancholy and made people merry and glad. Although it is possibly a flight of fancy to think so, there may be an unknown alchemy in the plant that does do this, as all parts of this herb were known to be beneficial. The leaves, besides being a pot-herb and used in salads, were also an ingredient in a 'cosmetic bath', which was a bath not only to cleanse, but to strengthen the body and beautify the skin.

Borage is also one of the bee plants, and the young leaves, which have a distinct cucumber flavour, are excellent in fruit drinks and claret cup.

Once the seed is sown in the spring and the plant is established, there will always be borage in the garden; and although it is an annual, it often flowers right through the winter. It is a charming little plant, growing demurely with its blue head slightly bowed like that of some medieval lady.

Borage

The flowers are five-pointed Madonna-blue stars, the colour often used by old masters to paint the robes of Christ's mother. This is the flower featured in old needlework, and it would be delightful to see it come back into favour. There is also a rare white-flowering variety.

The method for crystallizing borage flowers described in the following paragraph can be used for violets, mint leaves, carnation petals and tiny whole rosebuds. Rose petals may be preserved in this way too, or in the alternative way described in the section on Roses (page 127). A helpful hint is to buy a Fahrenheit thermometer for gauging the heat of the candying liquid.

CRYSTALLIZED FLOWERS

The quantities of sugar and water needed for crystallizing 2 heaped tablespoons of borage flowers, or 1 bunch of large violets, are 1 lb. of castor sugar and 1 cup of water.

Put the sugar and water in a saucepan over a steady heat and bring to the boil. Have the thermometer ready standing in a jug of hot water. Lift out and stand it in the saucepan until the syrup reaches 240 degrees. Put the thermometer back into the hot water and drop the dry flowers into the syrup, about 1 dozen at a time. Boil at 240 degrees or a little more for 1 minute. Lift out the flowers with a perforated spoon and lay them carefully on a sheet of aluminium foil. Place in a slightly warmed oven and leave to cool, turning once during the process.

Instead of throwing the left-over syrup away it is a good idea to use it in a caramel custard.

CARAMEL CUSTARD

Boil the syrup further until it turns to caramel, then pour into a fireproof dish turning it quickly to cover the bottom and sides. Make a custard with 2 eggs, 1 tablespoon of sugar, and ¾ pint of milk, and pour on to the caramel. Stand in a baking dish of water and cook in a moderate oven until set. It may be served chilled and topped with whipped cream decorated with crystallized flowers.

A COSMETIC BATH

(from 'The Toilet of Flora' in *The Scented Garden*, by E. S. Rohde)

Take 2 lb. of barley or bean-meal, 8 lb. of bran, and a few handfuls of borage leaves. Boil these ingredients in a sufficient quantity of spring water. Nothing cleanses and softens the skin like this bath.

Caraway Seed

Caraway (*Carum carvi*) is a biennial plant, one of the Umbelliferae. It is native to the Mediterranean shores and is now indigenous all over Europe. It is grown largely for the aromatic seeds, but the roots are also edible, being boiled and eaten like carrots. The German name for caraway is *Kümmel*, the well-known liqueur of this name having oil of caraway in its composition.

Caraway seed is very good for the digestion, and is the reason why it is traditionally included in, or eaten with, certain food. Florence White explains this very clearly in *Good English Food*:

'Roasted apples eaten with caraway comfits are a homely early eighteenth-century preventative of many of the ills that flesh is heir to.

'An old gentleman of over eighty wrote in 1714 that he had eaten a roasted apple with caraway comfits every night for fifty years, and had never suffered from constipation, gout, or stone or any other distemper incident to old age.

'The custom is a much older one, dating back to the time of ancient Greece and Rome, and is probably the origin of the old saying; "An apple a day keeps the doctor away."

'Apples are apt to cause flatulence, for which caraway seeds and comfits give relief, and it was the custom of our ancestors to serve a dish of baked apples and caraway comfits after a meal.'

There are many other virtues attributed to caraway: it was

put into love potions; and Dioscorides, the great Greek physician who lived in the first century A.D., prescribed it for 'girls of pale face'.

Caraway seed is used in breads, particularly rye. Certain cheeses are flavoured with caraway, and it is the ingredient which gives seed cake its name. Caraway seed also flavours pickles, soups, vegetables, and meat and fish dishes.

CARAWAY RICE RING AND TUNA FISH

A tasty, if expensive, meal for meatless days. The moulded rice looks colourful and attractive.

one 15-oz. tin tuna fish
2 oz. butter or margarine, and 2 extra tablespoons
1 heaped tablespoon plain flour
1 dessertspoon paprika
1 pint milk
1 lb. rice
1 dessertspoon caraway seeds
2 oz. red caviar
2 teaspoons parsley
salt and pepper

Melt 2 oz. butter in a saucepan, blend in the flour and paprika, and mix to a paste. Gradually add the milk, season with salt and pepper, and add the tuna. Keep hot.

Put the rice into a quantity of boiling salted water, and when cooked drain it in a colander, running some hot water over it to separate the grains. Shake well, turn into a bowl, fold in the extra butter (melted), and the caraway seeds, caviar, and parsley. Turn into a ring mould, press the rice in firmly, then unmould immediately on to a large platter. Pour some of the hot tuna into the centre of the ring, and the rest around it. Serve at once.

PINEAPPLE AND CHEESE IN THE SHELL

Cut a large ripe pineapple cleanly in half lengthwise through the green top, and scoop out the flesh, discarding the core. Chop the flesh into cubes, put into a bowl, and add 1 cup sugar and 1 tablespoon of sherry. Cover and leave for an hour or so. Chop ½ lb. mild Cheddar cheese into cubes and add to the pineapple, then stir in 1 tablespoon of caraway seed. Spoon the mixture into the pineapple shells, and chill.

SEED SPONGE CAKE

Seed cakes were made in some parts of England at least four hundred years ago, at the end of the wheat-growing season.

3 eggs, separated	1 tablespoon orange-flower water
5 oz. castor sugar	(from the chemist)
4 oz. self-raising flour	2 tablespoons water
1½ tablespoons cornflour	1 tablespoon caraway seed
1 dessertspoon butter	a pinch of salt

Beat the egg-whites until stiff and dry, and make a stiff meringue by gradually adding the sugar and beating until the grains are dissolved. Gently mix in the egg-yolks. Sift the flour, salt, and cornflour together three times and fold this lightly into the egg and sugar mixture. Heat together the butter, orange-flower water, and water, and fold it into the flour mixture at once together with the caraway seed. Pour into a well-greased and floured tin, sprinkle the top with castor sugar, and bake in a moderately hot oven (gas 6, electric 400°F.) for 20 minutes.

Cardamom Seed

Cardamom (*Amomum cardamomum*) is a perennial plant originating from India. It is valued for the small irregularly shaped seeds which have a strong, cool, eucalyptus-scented flavour. Cardamom is an ingredient in Indian curry powder blends, and in other forms of Indian cooking. It is also popular in Scandinavian cookery.

A delicious Indian pudding was prepared for us one day from some quite ordinary ingredients combined with exotic ones to give an exquisite appearance and distinctive flavour. It was simply a rice pudding called *Kheer*; the milk, rice, and sugar were soaked together, then cooked in a double saucepan with a grated carrot. When the rice was cooked, cracked cardamom seed was added, the rice mixture was put into a glass dish and covered with gossamer-thin sheets of pure silver, then finished with a pattern of shelled almonds shaved thinly. It was eaten cold, and the taste was cool and aromatic: a sensible dessert to eat in a hot country and probably following a spicy curry dish. The silver seemed to melt in the mouth, and in fact when we handled a tissue-wrapped bundle of silver sheets, which was produced to demonstrate the fine texture, it was so ephemeral that it appeared to float away. Only gentle and practised fingers could succeed in creating the finished effect we saw. In India, gold leaf is used as well for puddings on special occasions.

Cardamom seed is very hard and needs to be cracked by being pressed with a rolling pin before being used. Blend it into the curry powder, or put a teaspoon into a pastry mixture before adding the liquid; use it in gingerbread, in coffee cake, in fruit dishes, and in rice pudding. Crush a few seeds and put them in a small bowl to be handed with coffee crystals for black coffee.

ICED BEETROOT AND CARDAMOM SALAD

This method of cooking beetroots seems to preserve the goodness and flavour, and, as Mrs Beeton observes, without 'loss of their beautiful colour'.

Place 4 large beets in a dish and bake in a slow oven for about 3 hours. Cool slightly, peel and slice thinly. Sprinkle with sugar, a little salt, and 2 teaspoons cracked cardamom seed. Pour French dressing (page 158) over, and chill thoroughly.

BAKED PEARS AND CARDAMOM

When fruit is baked in the oven, especially in wine or in a liqueur, it has a better flavour than when cooked on top of the stove.

Peel, slice and core pears, lay them in a shallow ovenproof dish, sprinkle with sugar, and add 2 tablespoons wine or liqueur. (I have used Tia Maria, which has a chocolate flavour, successfully on one occasion.) Sprinkle with 2 teaspoons of cracked cardamom seed. Bake in a moderate oven (gas 4, electric 350°F.) until the pears are soft. Allow to cool. Serve with a little thick cream: the flavour of this dish must not be lost by being drowned in too much cream or custard.

CARDAMOM HONEY DRESSING

A delicious and nourishing dressing for fruit salad, halved melons, waffles, or corn cakes.

Beat ½ pint clear honey in an electric mixer until it is light in colour. Gradually add 2 tablespoons lemon juice and a few drops of orange-flower water. Stir in ½ teaspoon cracked cardamom seed. Keep in a screw-top glass jar.

Cayenne

Cayenne pepper (*Capsicum*) is the ground product from various species of dried capsicum or red chilli pepper. It is cultivated in the East Indies, Africa, and many other parts of the world, in temperate as well as tropical zones. This is an ornamental plant, bearing small, brilliant pods of vermilion fruit. An excellent culinary spice, cayenne also has digestive properties.

Cayenne pepper is extremely hot and so it must be used sparingly. A small amount is invaluable in cheese dishes, sauces, egg dishes, and with shellfish. Cayenne is stimulating and zestful, and is a classic ingredient in a Newburg Sauce.

NEWBURG SAUCE

3 tablespoons butter
3 tablespoons plain flour
1 teaspoon paprika
a pinch of cayenne
2 cups thin cream or top of the milk
3 egg-yolks, slightly beaten
1 tablespoon sherry
salt

Melt the butter in a saucepan. Blend in the flour, paprika, and cayenne. Add the cream gradually, stirring until the mixture thickens. Pour a little of this sauce on to the egg-yolks, mix well, and return the mixture to the saucepan. Add the sherry, and a pinch of salt. Carefully reheat, stirring constantly (do not boil). Add whatever shellfish you are serving – cooked lobster pieces, prawns, or scallops – and heat them through. Transfer to a hot dish and serve immediately with steaming rice; or serve with triangles of hot buttered toast.

EGG AND POTATO PIE

Peel and boil some potatoes and whip them until creamy with butter, milk, a little salt and pepper, and a grated onion. Spread thickly in a buttered ovenproof dish. Break an egg into a cup and slide it gently on to the potato; repeat, covering the potato with as many eggs as required. Mask the eggs with a little cream or top of the milk, and sprinkle with salt and cayenne. Bake in a medium-hot oven (gas 6, electric 380°F.) until the whites are set and the yolks are still soft-looking.

TOMATO DUMPLINGS

4 oz. self-raising flour
a walnut-sized piece of butter
1 dessertspoon grated cheese
¼ teaspoon salt
1 dessertspoon chopped parsley (optional)
6 tablespoons tomato juice
a pinch of cayenne

This is a delicious recipe from my neighbour Mrs R. E. Allen.

Sift the flour with the salt and cayenne, rub in the butter, add the cheese and, if liked, some chopped parsley. Stir in the tomato juice, making a very soft scone dough. Drop spoonfuls on top of a prepared favourite stew a little time before it is ready to serve (say 15 minutes), put the lid back on, and let the dumplings cook gently for 12 to 15 minutes.

CHEESE STRAWS

¼ lb. butter
¼ lb. plain flour
3 tablespoons grated cheese
a pinch of cayenne
salt
1 egg-yolk

Rub the butter, flour, and cheese together, season with salt and cayenne and add the egg-yolk. If the mixture is too stiff, moisten with a little water. Roll out and cut into strips, forming three or four of them into circles. Bake in a hot oven (gas 7, electric 400°F.) for about 15 minutes. When the cheese straws are cool slip them in bundles into the circles.

Celery Seed

Celery seed is the dried fruit of the celery plant (*Apium graveolens*), one of the Umbelliferae, thought to be native to Europe. However, it is said that originally it was the pot-herb known as smallage, which is wild celery: indeed, many of today's cultivated vegetables were once the simple pot-herbs of our forebears. Culpeper describes smallage in his *Complete Herbal* thus: 'The roots are about a finger thick, wrinkled, and sinking deep in the earth, of a white colour, from which spring many winged leaves of a yellow colour ... the roots, leaves, and seed are used.'

Mrs C. F. Leyel says that celery juice 'is an anti-acid tonic and stimulant rich in volatile oils and fruit sugar. It is a simple and effective remedy for some rheumatic complaints.' It is interesting to read from quite another source that celery has the property to help rheumatism. Here is a recipe from *Lotions and Potions*: 'Boil 1 oz. of celery seed in 1 pint of water until reduced to half. Strain, bottle and cork carefully. Take 1 teaspoonful twice a day in a little water for a fortnight. Repeat again if required.'

Celery seed is small and brownish, and has a potent taste. It is possibly one of the most popular flavourings on the spice shelf. It goes into tomato juice and seafood cocktails; in pickles and chutney; on top of breads and rolls; in soups, stews, fish dishes, and nearly all vegetable dishes; in white sauces and mayonnaise; and in cheese and herb-butter mixtures. Commercial celery salt is flavoured with ground celery seed, or with ground dried celery stems.

CABBAGE ASPIC

4 *cups finely shredded cabbage*
2 *cups chopped celery*
1 *red capsicum, thinly sliced*
1 *tablespoon celery seed*
4 *tablespoons gelatine*
1 *cup sugar*
4 *cups cold water*
2 *cups very hot water*
1 *cup cider vinegar*
salt
freshly ground pepper

Chervil

Green and glistening, this salad is a crisp and delicious accompaniment to a main meat course.

Put the 2 cups of very hot water (just off the boil) on to the gelatine and sugar, and stir until both are dissolved. Add the 4 cups of cold water and the vinegar, and leave until cool, but not set. Stir in the rest of the ingredients, and pour into a rinsed-out mould. When set, unmould on to a bed of fresh herbs or lettuce leaves.

AROMATIC SWEET POTATOES

Peel and slice 1 lb. sweet potatoes and arrange in a buttered ovenproof dish. Top with slices of rindless bacon and halved pineapple rings, and sprinkle with brown sugar, freshly ground pepper, and 2 teaspoons celery seed. Bake in a moderate oven (gas 4, electric 350°F.) for 40 or 45 minutes. Serve with meat casserole, grills, or baked veal.

SHARP MAYONNAISE

To be eaten with cold meat.

Mix together 1 cup mayonnaise, ¼ cup prepared horseradish, and 2 teaspoons celery seed.

Chervil

Chervil (*Anthriscus cerefolium*) is a small, twelve-inch-high biennial herb of the Umbelliferae family, with delicate fernlike leaves. Its rather nondescript appearance is misleading as it has great culinary value, and is well worth growing. Chervil is native to eastern Europe, self-sowing easily in cool climates. It is grown successfully in semi-shade in summer, but it does like the winter sun, a factor which presents a problem. If it is planted where annual herbs will protect it through the hot months, by the time winter comes the annuals are out of the way and it then benefits from the sunshine. When dried it holds its aroma and green colour well.

Chervil

This herb is particularly suitable for growing in a pot or trough. A good spot is the kitchen window-sill where it is within easy reach to pick and cut up for salads, mashed potato, and especially scrambled egg; its nearness is appreciated for early breakfasts. Always pick the leaves from the outside, as with parsley, allowing it to keep on growing from the centre.

The leaves have a fresh yet spicy taste, delicately scented with aniseed, and although it certainly does not take the place of parsley, it may, with great advantage, be used instead, adding a different flavour to familiar food. It is excellent with omelettes and in soups. Other suggestions are:

A tossed French salad with as much chopped chervil as you can spare sprinkled on the top before serving.

Diced cold potato mixed together with a light mayonnaise dressing and a generous amount of chervil.

Iced tomato soup garnished with thin slices of lemon and finely chopped chervil.

Haricot beans served piping hot with a piquant sauce, and chervil added at the last.

Nicolas Culpeper aptly describes chervil in his *Complete Herbal* written in the seventeenth century:

'The garden chervil doth at first somewhat resemble parsley, but after it is better grown the leaves are cut in and jagged, resembling hemlock, being a little hairy, and of a whitish green colour, sometimes turning reddish in the summer, with the stalks also; it riseth a little above half a foot high, bearing white flowers in spiked tufts, which turn into long and round seeds pointed at the ends, and blackish when they are ripe ...'

POTATO SOUP

1 lb. potatoes	1 dessertspoon flour blended with milk
1 onion	
chervil	a little cream
1 pint stock or water	salt and pepper

Wash and slice the potato and onion, and simmer on the stove in the liquid until the vegetables are soft.

Chervil

Rub through a sieve and return to the stove with the blended flour. Bring to the boil, and pour into hot soup plates. Add thin cream, fried *croûtons* and 1 teaspoon chopped chervil to each serving.

SPINACH SOUP

2 pints beef stock
1 pint cooked spinach, sieved or put through a blender
1 or more eggs for each person
a little cream
chervil
salt and pepper

Put the puréed spinach into a saucepan with the beef stock. Heat, adding salt and pepper to taste. Have ready the eggs which have been boiled for 4 minutes and shelled. Serve the hot soup in individual bowls with a whole egg, a dessertspoon of cream, and a generous sprinkling of chervil.

SEAFOOD SALAD

3 cups fish, cooked and flaked
1 cup shelled prawns
1 bottle oysters, drained
1 dessertspoon chopped chives (or 2 dessertspoons chopped shallots)
2 tomatoes, peeled and diced
1 cucumber, peeled and diced
½ cup mayonnaise
1 tablespoon lemon juice
1 tablespoon thick cream
chervil
salt and pepper

Toss all ingredients together (except the chervil) and chill in the refrigerator. Serve in a bowl lined with crisp lettuce leaves, strewing the top until green with the chervil.

ICED AVOCADO AND CHERVIL

This makes a refreshing accompaniment to a main dish. Slice 2 peeled and stoned avocadoes lengthwise into slender pieces. Marinate in lemon juice seasoned with salt and freshly ground pepper. To serve, sprinkle with plenty of chervil and arrange on a bed of cracked ice.

HARICOT BEANS WITH TOMATOES

This is excellent in the winter when fresh vegetables are often scarce and is quite sufficient on its own with the main meat course.

1 lb. haricot beans	2 crushed cloves garlic
1 lb. tomatoes	1 dessertspoonful brown sugar
4 shallots	2 tablespoons chervil
4 oz. butter or margarine	salt and pepper

Pour boiling water over the beans and soak them overnight. Simmer in salted water until soft (about 1½ hours). Drain.

Wash the shallots and cut them up finely leaving as much of the green part as possible for colour and flavour. Put them with the garlic into a frying pan with the melted fat. Simmer gently until soft. Peel and chop the tomatoes and with the sugar, salt and pepper add to the frying pan. Cook a little longer, then pour the purée on to the beans and heat through. Just before serving stir in the chervil.

To vary, emulate the famous dish cassoulet, which originates from the rich farming country of south-west France, by adding to the beans ½ lb. fried, lean bacon cut into pieces, or 1 lb. of sliced garlic sausage. Pour the mixture into a casserole, top with buttered breadcrumbs and brown slowly in the oven.

Chicory

Chicory (*Cichorium intybus*), or succory as it was once called, is regarded more as a vegetable or pot-herb, although it is delicious when a tablespoon of the finely shredded leaves are added to a lettuce salad. The leaves have a slightly bitter yet pleasant taste, and are esteemed for their health-giving properties.

Culpeper says of it: 'A handful of the leaves or roots, boiled in wine or water, and drank fasting, drives forth choleric and phlegmatic humours.'

The plant can grow to over six feet high, and in the autumn the china-blue flowers are carried on long spires, making a welcome show of colour in the herb garden at this time of year.

Chicory

As well as having medicinal uses, the roots are dried and ground to mix with coffee, and may be boiled like parsnips and eaten as a vegetable.

Plant the seed in the spring and give this large plant plenty of room to grow.

CHICORY AND EGGS

This is an up-to-date version of a three-hundred-year-old recipe.

Blanch chicory leaves for 5 minutes in boiling water. Drain and squeeze out the moisture. Cut them with a knife and put in a saucepan with a little stock and a bunch of chopped savoury herbs (marjoram, parsley and thyme for instance) and simmer for $\frac{1}{2}$ hour. Thicken with a little blended cornflour and turn on to a serving dish. Keep hot while poaching the eggs to lay upon the cooked chicory. Serve at once.

CHICORY SALAD

1 lettuce
1 chicory leaf
1 dozen stoned black olives
8 anchovy fillets
4 hard-boiled eggs
1 cup diced celery
4 peeled tomatoes, cut into quarters
1 tablespoon chopped chervil and chives in equal parts
French dressing
a clove of garlic

Chop the fresh, dry chicory leaf and put with the torn-up lettuce in a bowl that has been rubbed with a cut clove of garlic. Add all ingredients except the herbs, anchovies and hard-boiled eggs, and toss well. Arrange the halved eggs with an anchovy on each one on top of the salad, and sprinkle with herbs. Serve with cold meat and French bread for lunch, or alfresco on a hot summer night.

Chilli Powder

Chilli powder may be a mixture of dried ground chilli peppers, aromatic seeds, spices, and herbs, or it may be the ground peppers unmixed; the flavour differs with the manufacturers' formulas, and varies from mildly hot to very hot. The quantity of chilli powder given in these recipes will vary with the brand you buy. At first it is better to use a little less than too much.

Cayenne, cumin, and oregano are often added in the preparation of the blend. The best and hottest chilli powder comes from small bright red chillis known as bird's-eye peppers. Originally this spice came from Mexico, where the Aztecs introduced it to the conquering Spaniards in the sixteenth century.

The aroma of the powder is fiercely peppery, the colour being a rust red and the flavour hot and glowing. Its best-known use is in Chilli con Carne, a Mexican dish, but it has become indispensable in the making of certain sauces and in the blending of some curry powders.

When used prudently, chilli powder sharpens the flavour of egg dishes, soups, and vegetables, and is particularly good as a flavouring in baked beans.

It once took me two days to prepare Boston Baked Beans for a barbecue, mixing triple quantities of haricot beans, salt pork, and molasses. The result was a sweet and sticky mess. A quick and easy dish using tinned baked beans and a sauce well spiced with chilli powder has been an excellent standby since then. Here is the recipe.

BARBECUE BAKED BEANS

2 1-lb. tins baked beans
4 *medium to large tomatoes*
2 *onions*
1 *clove of garlic*
1 *tablespoon brown sugar*
2 tablespoons butter or margarine
1 teaspoon mustard powder
½ teaspoon chilli powder
salt

Pour boiling water on to the tomatoes, skin them, and chop

coarsely. Peel and slice the onions and garlic and cook in the melted butter until soft. Add the brown sugar, mustard powder, chilli powder, and some salt to taste. Cook until mushy (about 10 minutes), add the baked beans, and cook a little longer. Serves 8.

CHILLI CON CARNE

A fiery dish to take the place of curry for a change. Legend says that the Aztecs showed the *conquistadores* how to make it.

2 lb. lean steak, chopped into cubes	2 onions, peeled and chopped
	2 cloves of garlic, chopped
1¼ lb. dried red kidney beans or 2 10-oz. tins	1 teaspoon chilli powder
	2 tablespoons plain flour
1 large tin tomatoes	1 teaspoon oregano
3 tablespoons vegetable oil	1 teaspoon cumin seed
	2 teaspoons salt

If dried beans are used soak them overnight, and then simmer them in the same water until almost tender. Strain and put on one side.

Heat the oil in an enamelled fireproof dish or a thick saucepan, add the onion and garlic, and cook until soft. Add the chilli powder and meat, turning the meat until it is evenly browned. Blend in the flour, then add tomatoes (including any liquid), oregano, and cumin. Cover, and simmer for 1 hour. Add the beans and salt, and cook for a further 15 minutes.

Chilli con Carne (meaning chilli with meat) is improved if made a day in advance: the spices will have truly permeated the meat, gravy, and beans. Serve hot, with a crisp green salad and some ice-cold beer. For special occasions a wine from Alsace, Gewürztraminer, is suggested: its powerful bouquet is a fit companion for the hot Chilli con Carne.

MEXICAN GUACAMOLE

The avocado pear, as well as chilli powder, was once a favourite of the Aztecs.

Mash one ripe avocado pear until creamy, incorporate one small grated onion, one small, peeled, finely chopped tomato, a few drops of olive oil, and a pinch each of oregano, salt and chilli powder. Place in a dish, with the stone of the avocado embedded in the mixture to prevent discoloration, and chill. Serve on a large lettuce leaf, as a savoury dip, with potato chips or plain biscuits.

Chives

Chives (*Allium schoenoprasum*) belong to the same family as the onion, leek, garlic and shallot. The thin, grass-like leaves have a delicate taste of onion, and are generally used to flavour cream cheese, salads and omelettes.

Chives make an attractive border. The flowers look like little mauve pincushions, and are charming in a mixed posy.

If both the leaves and the flowers are picked continuously, the plant grows more vigorously and has a better flavour. Chives may suddenly die out and disappear, so divide the bulbs in the autumn to prevent overcrowding, water them in dry weather, and top-dress twice a year with old poultry humus.

If you are raising the plant from seed, sow in the spring. It grows successfully on a kitchen window-sill, and then has the added advantage of being within easy reach when needed.

Chives and cream cheese have an affinity. Chop the chives finely and mash them into the cream cheese with salt, pepper, a little cream and a squeeze of lemon juice. Spread on savouries and in sandwiches or pat into a mound in the centre of a serving dish and surround with biscuits; supply a knife and let your guests help themselves to this savoury mixture either as a before-dinner appetizer, or to eat afterwards.

Another suggestion is to add a tablespoon of chopped chives to mashed potato, particularly when it accompanies grilled chops, steak, or crumbed cutlets. The uses of this herb are many and varied, especially to the imaginative cook.

Cucumber and chives combine well, and the first recipe to follow – Creamed Cucumber – is excellent.

CREAMED CUCUMBER

2 *cucumbers*
1 *tablespoon chopped chives*
1 *cup white sauce*
salt and pepper

Peel the cucumbers, cut into cubes, put into boiling water and cook a few minutes. Drain. Make a white sauce with 1½ tablespoons of butter, 2 level tablespoons of flour and 1 cup of milk. Stir in the cucumber, chives, salt and pepper. Heat through and serve hot.

FRENCH OMELETTE WITH CHIVES

Those who own a correct omelette pan, heavy with a flat bottom and shallow with sloping sides, are fortunate; however, a successful omelette may still be made in an ordinary frying pan. Experienced cooks say that one omelette should never contain more than six eggs; I find it easier to make several, one for each person, unless making the omelette for two people, in which case six eggs may be used.

3 eggs
1 oz. butter
chives, salt and pepper

Dissolve the butter over a medium heat. Meanwhile, break the eggs into a bowl and whisk well but lightly. Season with salt and pepper, add two tiny cubes of butter and the chives.

When the butter is sizzling gently, see that it is distributed evenly over the pan, and pour in the eggs. With a knife quickly lift up the sides of the omelette all round the pan allowing the mixture to run underneath. Do this several times, and cut it once across the middle. The bottom of the omelette should be set and a golden brown, the top creamy and not quite cooked. Lift the omelette with an egg slice, fold it over, slide it on to a hot plate and serve immediately.

FISH PIE WITH HERBS

3 cups cooked flaked fish
1½ cups white sauce
1 tablespoon chopped chives
1 dessertspoon chopped walnuts
salt, pepper, grated nutmeg
1 dessertspoon chopped parsley

Stir the fish into the white sauce. Season with salt, pepper and nutmeg. Put into a fireproof dish and top with herbs and walnuts. Brown in a medium oven and serve with slices of lemon and very thin brown bread and butter.

Cinnamon

This spice (*Cinnamomum zeylanicum*, one of the Lauraceae), which comes from a tree native to Ceylon and Malabar, has been highly esteemed from remote times for its preservative and medicinal qualities, and as a flavouring for food and beverages.

When the trees are grown commercially the tender bark is peeled from the numerous long, slender shoots, and it curls into quills or sticks which are then dried in the sun. The fragrance of the bark comes from an essential oil, oil of cinnamon, which has valuable medicinal uses.

The dried bark from a cassia tree is also known as cinnamon, and is similar in flavour and appearance.

Cinnamon is used either whole or powdered. Ground cinnamon mixed with sugar on hot buttered toast is an old favourite; buttered tea cake strewn with sugar and cinnamon is always eaten down to the last delectable spiced crumb. Ground cinnamon gives liveliness to milk puddings, mulled wines, chutneys, and cakes, and to various vegetables and stewed fruits. Combined with other spices it is a traditional ingredient in Christmas cakes, mince pies, and Christmas puddings, and is also one of the spices that go into the blending of curry powder.

Cinnamon sticks are used in a variety of ways: stirring black coffee with a piece of cinnamon gives it an Eastern aura, while on a bleak night a hot rum toddy flavoured with a little sugar and a twist of lemon peel and spiked with aromatic cinnamon sticks is most comforting, especially after a long journey.

In 1815 a tooth-powder was made by mixing '$\frac{1}{2}$ oz. powdered cinnamon and $\frac{1}{2}$ oz. well-prepared chalk well together'. This is one of the 'receipts' in *Lotions and Potions*.

SWEET-SOUR HARICOT BEANS

- 1 lb. haricot beans
- 2 pints water
- 1½ oz. demerara sugar
- ¼ cup cider vinegar
- 1 tablespoon golden syrup
- 2 teaspoons salt
- a piece of cinnamon stick

This is an excellent dish to serve with meat, or with crisp bacon for breakfast.

Wash the beans, cover with the water, and soak overnight. Do not change the water. Simmer next day for 30 minutes or until the beans are soft. Add the rest of the ingredients, and cook slowly with the lid off, stirring occasionally, for a further 30 minutes or until tender. Serve piping hot.

TREACLE TART

As old-fashioned as caraway comfits and syllabubs, or pot-pourri and beeswax candles, this delightful tart is as welcome today as it ever was. A sprinkling of cinnamon over the top, although not in all the traditional recipes, is a pleasing addition. The pastry for this sweet is excellent when made with fine wholemeal flour instead of refined white flour.

Short pastry
- 8 oz. wholemeal flour
- 1 teaspoon baking powder
- a pinch of salt
- 2 oz. butter or margarine
- ¼ cup cold water

Filling
- 3 tablespoons golden syrup
- 1 dessertspoon lemon juice
- grated lemon rind
- 3 tablespoons soft white breadcrumbs
- 1 teaspoon ground cinnamon

Sift the flour, baking powder and salt. Rub in the butter. Add enough water to make a stiff dough. Roll out on a floured board. Line a greased flat pie-plate with the pastry, pricking well all over.

For the filling, measure the syrup into a saucepan with a hot tablespoon (this makes the measuring easier), add the lemon juice, grated rind, and breadcrumbs. Warm slightly over low heat, pour into the pastry case, sprinkle with the cinnamon, and bake in a moderate oven (gas 4, electric 350–75 °F.) for 25 minutes. Serve cold with cream.

DEVONSHIRE JUNKET

An old recipe from *Good English Food* by Florence White, this has been altered slightly to suit ingredients available today.

Mix together in a bowl 1 tablespoon sugar, 1 tablespoon brandy or rum, ½ teaspoon ground cinnamon, and 1 teaspoon rennet. Pour on to these 1 pint warm milk. Allow to set, then spread ¼ pint whipped cream over the top and sprinkle with sugar. 'When well made, junket should cut into smooth shiny slices like jelly. Unlike jelly, it will set better and more quickly in a room of ordinary temperature than a cold larder.'

FLAMING BANANAS

A lighted dessert is always exciting. This recipe is delicious as well.

Allow 2 bananas for each person. Peel and halve, place in a shallow fireproof dish, sprinkle with lemon juice, strew with sugar and cinnamon, and dot liberally with butter. Place under a medium-hot grill, and when soft and golden bring to the table, pour over 2 oz. rum, and ignite it.

RICH SPICED CHRISTMAS CAKE

7 oz. plain flour
1 oz. self-raising flour
½ lb. butter
3 oz. demerara sugar
½ cup best honey
5 eggs
1 level teaspoon of each of these: salt, ground cinnamon, ground cloves, ground allspice, nutmeg
juice and grated rind of 1 lemon
¼ lb. each of these: glacé cherries, sultanas, stoned raisins, crystallized pineapple, glacé figs, mixed peel, crystallized papaw (if available), shelled almonds
1 sherry glass of rum (or the same amount of orange juice)

Prepare the fruit, halving the nuts and cherries and chopping the bigger fruit into small cubes. Sift the flours and spices together, and mix a small portion of this sifted spiced flour with the fruit. Cream the butter and sugar, add the honey, the eggs one at a time, and the lemon juice and grated rind. Fold in the sifted spiced flour, then the fruit, and lastly the rum or orange juice. Put into an 8-inch baking tin which has been lined with two thicknesses of brown paper (the inner layer oiled with butter). Bake in a slow oven (gas 1, electric 300°F.) for 3 to 4 hours. Weight when cooked is about 4 lb.

Cloves

Whole cloves (*Eugenia caryophyllata*) are the dried flower-buds of an aromatic evergreen tree that is native to the Molucca Islands and is grown today in many hot countries. The pungent clove, either whole or ground, has become a necessary flavouring in a number of dishes. The volatile oil of cloves, a powerful antiseptic, is familiar to everyone.

The name clove is derived from the Latin word *clavus*, meaning nail, which the clove resembles in form.

A deliciously scented clove orange hung in the clothes closet was extremely popular a few centuries ago for repelling insects (see page 169). Held to the nostrils, a clove orange allayed the more offensive odours of the times. 'It is not surprising that Cardinal Wolsey, when he ventured either into the lower regions of his own residence or risked the pervasive odours of the streets of London, commonly carried a spice-ball ...' (*A Tudor Tragedy*, by Lacey Baldwin Smith).

Whole cloves are used as a flavouring in many kinds of preserves, mulled wines, stewed fruits, meat dishes, and soups. For stews or soups simmer with the other ingredients a whole onion studded with cloves and remove it before serving. Drop a clove into the hollowed-out centre of a cooking-apple, pack with butter and brown sugar, and bake in a moderate oven (gas 4, electric 350°F.) until tender.

When boiling fresh salt pork add to the water a few cloves, together with some peppercorns, a pinch of thyme, and a bay leaf. Simmer for about 2 hours, allow to cool in the water, drain, and keep chilled. The delicate texture of the pork permeated with the herbs and spices is often preferred to bacon.

A baked leg of ham, crumbed and studded with whole cloves and tinned pineapple, is a traditional favourite. Clove-spiced hot pineapple cut in slices and eaten with barbecued meat or served with pork or ham is excellent: stud a carefully peeled pineapple with cloves and cook on a rotisserie (if you have one in your stove), or spike through the centre with a long skewer and turn slowly over the barbecue coals. Baste with melted butter and orange juice until well glazed and heated throughout.

Ground cloves are included in numerous recipes, such as fruit cake, buns, mincemeat, milk puddings, and various sauces and vegetable dishes.

BEET BORTSCH

Make a good rich stock with 2 lb. beef bones and a knuckle of veal covered with water, 1 medium-sized carrot, 1 parsnip, 2 tomatoes (chopped), salt, a little sugar, peppercorns, a bay leaf, thyme, and an onion stuck with cloves.

After it has simmered for 2 or 3 hours strain it and return it to the pot, adding 4 raw grated beetroots. Simmer for 10 minutes. The quantity should now be from 3 to 4 pints.

In summer put the soup into a bowl in the refrigerator. If it does not jell overnight, dissolve gelatine in some hot water, stir into the soup, and chill. Serve jellied and icy cold with a spoonful of cream on each serving, and a dusting of ground cloves.

In winter omit the gelatine, add chopped frankfurters, and serve hot, perhaps with sour cream.

Vatroushki should be eaten with Bortsch: Tania, a friend of Russian extraction, has given her recipe, and having eaten these delicious little pies in her house I can warmly recommend them. They may accompany other vegetable soups or winter stews.

VATROUSHKI

Make your favourite short pastry, or the following: sift together 2 oz. self-raising flour, 4 oz. plain flour, a pinch of salt, and 1 dessertspoon sugar. Rub in 4 oz. butter or margarine, add cold water, and mix to a stiff dough. Now mix together ½ lb. cream cheese, 1 egg, 1 tablespoon sugar, a pinch of salt, and 2 tablespoons plain flour. Roll the pastry fairly thinly and cut out circles with a teacup or large glass. Place a spoonful of filling in the centre of each pastry circle, and fold into envelopes, pinching to secure. Brush each with beaten white of egg and bake on a tray for about 20 minutes in a moderate oven (gas 4, electric 350–75 °F.).

FESTIVE HAM

This recipe for garnishing a ham was given to me by a friend, Mrs R. R. Beck. The garnish may be applied either to cooked fresh ham or to tinned ham; it gives the meat an attractive, mouth-watering appearance and adds a delightful flavour.

If using a tinned ham, remove it carefully from the tin and put on a large plate or board. Remove every vestige of gelatine coating, and score the top deeply in a diamond pattern. With floured hands gently rub and pat flour all over the surface until it is quite dry, then stud the centre of each diamond with cloves.

Open a tin of pineapple rings, and drain them. Put the juice into a saucepan to heat, together with a generous portion of butter. (For the largest ham, 2 big tins of pineapple will be needed, and $\frac{1}{2}$ lb. butter.)

Make a mixture of dry breadcrumbs, flour, brown sugar, and some dry mustard, add enough hot pineapple mixture to make a thick paste, and spread a portion all over the top and sides of the ham. Lift it into a baking dish lined with buttered foil, put into a hot oven (gas 6–7, electric 400°F.) and let it heat through for 10 to 15 minutes. Remove from the oven, and with a knife or spatula spread the remaining paste on the top and sides.

Spear glacé cherries with wooden picks, putting one through each pineapple ring and on to the ham. Do this in a pleasing pattern around the sides first, then on the top, with the remaining cherries clustered together.

Return the ham to the oven for 20 minutes, allowing the coating to become crusty, then during the last 20 minutes baste frequently with the pineapple and butter, which must be kept bubbling on the stove. When all the liquid has been used, remove the ham from the oven and allow it to cool.

APPLE PUDDING

This is essentially a family pudding; it is a simple recipe, and nourishing. The quantity given is quite large, so there should be enough for 'seconds'. Have plenty of cream on the table.

Peel, slice, and core enough cooking apples to cover the bottom of a buttered baking dish thickly; add 4 or 5 whole cloves and 2 tablespoons seedless raisins, sprinkle with lemon juice, and strew with sugar. Pour over this a batter made with 2 cups plain flour, a pinch of salt, ½ cup sugar, 2 eggs, and 1 pint milk. Bake in a moderate oven (gas 4, electric 350°F.) for 1 hour.

Coriander Seed

Coriander (*Coriandrum sativum*) is an annual with pink-tinged, delicately lacy flowers. It is one of the Umbelliferae family, native to southern Europe and the Near East, and grows to two feet in height. It is one of the oldest herbs known to man. In the Bible the seed is likened to manna, tasting 'like wafers made with honey' (Exodus 16.31). Today it is grown in many parts of the world for its aromatic seeds, which must be allowed to ripen before being used as they are unpleasant when fresh.

Coriander was said by many of the early herbalists to associate well with chervil and dill, which blossom at the same time; this suggestion is also probably intended to carry out the interesting theory that certain plants are sympathetic to each other, one strengthening the other with special properties, perhaps by giving off an odour unpleasant to insects which would otherwise attack the vulnerable plant growing next to it; in return, this plant would contain qualities lacking in the other.

Coriander seeds are small, slightly oval, and bleached-

Coriander Seed

looking, with an agreeable spicy flavour. Sow the seeds in the spring, when the plants will soon grow to about two feet. As the seeds have the power of remaining fertile for up to five years, there is no need to worry over fresh supplies for planting. When the flowers have fallen, collect the ripe seed and store in an airtight jar: the fragrance improves with keeping.

The fragrant seeds are an ingredient in both curry powder and pot-pourri, and are often added to give a spicy flavour to food. A teaspoon of crushed seeds gives a subtle undertone to casseroles and soups.

ARABIAN STUFFED CAPSICUMS

12 *medium-sized green capsicums*
2 *cups stock (may be made with 2 soup cubes)*
2 *cups cooked, chopped lamb, or 1 lb. minced steak*
2 *cups cooked rice*
2 *tablespoons skinned, slivered almonds*
2 *onions, chopped*
2 *teaspoons crushed coriander seed*
½ *teaspoon ground cinnamon*
2 *tomatoes, peeled and diced*
1 *tablespoon chopped olives*
salt and pepper

Prepare the capsicums for stuffing by removing a piece from the top of each and scooping out the seeds. Mix together the lamb, rice, onion, almonds, coriander seed, cinnamon, tomato and olives, seasoning with a little salt and pepper. Stuff the capsicums, place in a baking dish, replace capsicum tops, cover with the stock, and bake in a moderate oven (gas 4, electric 350°F.) for 1 hour, basting frequently. If any meat mixture is left over, form it into balls and put them in the dish too.

BAKED VEAL CHOPS

Pound 2 cloves of garlic and 2 teaspoons coriander seed together, and mix with breadcrumbs. Dip chops in flour, egg and seasoned breadcrumbs, put in a baking dish with a little fat and the grated rind of ½ lemon. Cook in a moderate oven until brown and crisp.

Crumbed bananas may, with advantage, be added to the baking dish 15 minutes before serving.

Coriander Seed

CORIANDER HONEY CAKES

- 1 lb. honey
- ¼ lb. butter
- 1 lb. plain flour
- 4 tablespoons milk
- 1 teaspoon bicarbonate of soda
- 2 teaspoons crushed coriander seed

Put the honey and butter together in a saucepan and heat till bubbling. Cool a little, and pour into a bowl. Sift the flour and soda into the honey mixture, add the milk, then the crushed coriander seed. Chill, then turn on to a floured surface, form into cakes, and bake on greased and floured trays in a moderately hot oven (gas 6–7, electric 400°F.) for 15 minutes. Allow to cool on trays. Store in containers.

CORIANDER APPLE CRUMBLE

Cover the bottom of a buttered shallow ovenproof dish with peeled, sliced cooking apples, sprinkle with 1 tablespoon brown sugar and 1 teaspoon ground cinnamon. In a bowl rub together until crumbly 1 cup plain flour, ½ cup brown sugar, and ¼ lb. butter. Press and smooth this on top of the apples, then sprinkle with crushed coriander seed (try 1 teaspoon to begin with, and increase the amount next time you make this dessert, if you wish). Bake in a moderate oven (gas 4, electric 350°F.) for about 30 minutes. Serve hot or cold with cream.

SPICED TEA CAKE

- 1 tablespoon butter
- 4 oz. sugar
- 1 egg
- ½ pint milk
- 4 oz. self-raising flour
- 1 apple peeled and sliced thinly
- 1 dessertspoon pounded coriander seed
- a little sugar
- nutmeg

Cream the butter and sugar. Add the egg and beat well. Gently fold in the sifted flour and milk alternately.

Smear a cake tin with butter and then a dusting of flour. (This prevents the cake from sticking.) Lay the sliced apple in the bottom of the tin, and sprinkle with sugar, nutmeg and pounded coriander seed. Pour the batter over and bake in a moderate oven until cooked, about ½ hour. Carefully loosen the cake from the sides of the tin, and turn on to a plate or wire-cooler. It is delicious when hot, but may be eaten cold with thick cream.

MARMALADE FLAVOURED WITH CORIANDER

4 *oranges*
2 *lemons*
6 *cups water*
4 *lb. sugar*
1 *tablespoon crushed coriander seed*

Cut up the oranges and lemons and soak in water for 12 hours. Bring to the boil and put in the coriander seed tied in a muslin bag. When the peel is tender slowly add the warmed sugar, and boil until the mixture sets. Remove the muslin bag before putting the marmalade in jars.

The coriander seed will impart a spicy fragrance to the usually prosaic marmalade.

Cumin Seed

Cumin (*Cuminum cyminum*) is a small annual sun-loving herb, native to Egypt. It belongs to the Umbelliferae family. The pale pink flowers are followed by parchment-coloured seeds, the flavour of which almost holds the key to the pungent taste of curry powder. Some say that this seed resembles caraway in flavour; the seeds of both are very aromatic, but to my mind so essentially different that one could not easily replace the other. Cumin is mentioned in the Bible, the seed having been valued for the digestion, as well as for culinary purposes, for many centuries.

Cumin seed is used mainly in the blending of curry powder, chilli powder, and in flavouring dishes from the Near and Middle East. A teaspoon or two of the mildly hot seed gives an eastern flavour to food: it is often used in rye bread; in pickles and chutney; in rice, cabbage, and bean dishes; in meat dishes; and to mash into cottage cheese with a little lemon juice for a spread or dip.

Cumin Seed

TURKISH CUCUMBERS

4 *cucumbers*	1 *teaspoon salt*
1 *carton yoghurt*	1 *tablespoon wine vinegar*
1 *clove of garlic, finely chopped*	1 *teaspoon cumin seed*
	1 *teaspoon chopped mint*

Soak the garlic, salt and vinegar together. Strain. Peel the cucumbers and slice them thinly lengthwise. Put the yoghurt in a bowl and stir in gradually the strained vinegar. Add the cumin seed. Pour the dressing over the cucumbers, sprinkle with mint, and serve slightly chilled.

LAMB SHANKS ARMENIAN

6 *lamb shanks*	1 *teaspoon black peppercorns*
2 *tablespoons plain flour*	1 *tablespoon lemon juice*
2 *cloves of garlic, finely chopped*	1 *dill cucumber, sliced*
1 *onion, chopped*	3 *cups tomato juice*
1 *capsicum, chopped*	*salt*
2 *teaspoons cumin seed*	

Roll the shanks in the flour and place in a large casserole with the other ingredients. Put the lid on, and bake in a slow oven (gas ½–1, electric 275–300°F.) for 2½ hours. Serve hot with rice and plenty of the savoury liquid.

CUMIN AND ROSE-GERANIUM DROPS

6 *oz. butter*	*rose-geranium jelly (page 26)*
8 *oz. sugar*	*or other preserve*
2 *eggs*	*a pinch of salt*
12 *oz. self-raising flour*	2 *teaspoons cumin seed*

Cream the butter and sugar, beat in the eggs one at a time, fold in the sifted flour and salt, and add the cumin seed. Form into small balls with the hands, roll in sugar, make a depression in the centre of each, and fill with rose-geranium jelly. Bake in a moderate oven (gas 5, electric 375°F.). Cool on a tray and store in an airtight container.

Curry Powder

The word 'curry' immediately brings to mind spicy and colourful dishes from sun-drenched Eastern countries where 'the dawn comes up like thunder' and on the air is the sound of 'tinkly temple-bells'.

In these countries, with their hot climates, a way of preparing food has been evolved that is suitable for the comfortable and healthy functioning of the body: it is said, for instance, that many of the hotter spices have a purifying effect on the intestines, and also that in humid, muggy weather curries help to 'air-condition' the body.

Curry powder is not one spice but a blend of many spices which when combined with food gives it a unique flavour. In India each family grinds its own choice of aromatic seeds nearly every day. Flavours vary considerably from mild, medium and sweet to very hot, all depending on which spices, and how many, are used in each blend. Instead of a powder, curry paste is sometimes preferred, in which case the prepared powder, perhaps with different spices and herbs added, is usually moistened with vinegar, pulverized garlic and vegetable oil, then cooked gently for a few minutes and sealed down.

Curry blends vary widely in different countries: Indonesian curry is fiercer as a rule than Indian curry, which to my mind, although hot, is extremely aromatic.

Chicken, rabbit, meat, fish, shellfish, vegetables or hard-boiled eggs can be the main ingredient of a curry dish.

INDIAN CURRY

Accompaniments: Plenty of carefully cooked rice accompanies a curry, as well as relishes, which may number from three or four dishes to a great number. The traditional few are mango chutney, grated fresh coconut, or desiccated coconut, shredded Bombay duck (which is a tasty cured fish), and Indian mint sauce, a refreshing and delicious combination of

Curry Powder

mint leaves and an onion minced together. Fresh coriander leaves are a popular garnish for a curry.

Curry Powder: It is interesting to blend your own curry powder and to determine, yourself, the degree of heat and nuances of flavour. The recipe given here is intended to serve as a guide. Turmeric may be omitted and the same quantity of paprika used in its place, some people preferring the taste and colour. A little-known aromatic seed which is essential in the preparation of a curry blend is fenugreek. The small irregularly-shaped seeds are light golden-brown in colour, with a pleasantly bitter flavour and a warm, spicy scent.

An electric blender, grinding machine, or pestle and mortar may be used for the mixing and grinding of the powder and seeds. If desired, start from the beginning with the whole spice instead of the ground product: however, most spices bought already ground are simpler to use, and if the quality is good the result is satisfactory.

1 dessertspoon ground cinnamon	1 teaspoon chilli powder
1 teaspoon ground cloves	1 tablespoon ground coriander
1 dessertspoon ground ginger	1 tablespoon turmeric
1 dessertspoon fenugreek seed	1 dessertspoon cumin seed
1 dessertspoon mustard seed	2 teaspoons cardamom seed

Grind and blend all ingredients together. Keep in an airtight jar. A few whole cloves may be added – they help to perfume the blend deliciously.

MEAT CURRY

Ghee, which is clarified butter, is now available and is recommended for frying the ingredients, although groundnut oil may be used instead.

1 lb. trimmed beef or lamb, cut into cubes	2 or 3 tomatoes, chopped
	2 teaspoons salt
3 tablespoons ghee or groundnut oil	1 to 2 tablespoons curry powder
1 onion, chopped	2 tablespoons plain flour
4 cloves of garlic, chopped	$\frac{1}{4}$ pint stock
1 apple, chopped	1 tablespoon golden syrup
2 inches ginger root, peeled and sliced	1 lemon, cut in half

Curry Powder

Heat the ghee or oil in a frying pan, and add the onion, garlic, apple and ginger root. Fry gently until softened. Add the tomato, cook a little longer, then stir in the salt and curry powder. Fry for a few minutes. Transfer the contents of the frying pan to a heavy saucepan, add the meat and flour, and cook till brown. Gradually pour in the stock, then stir in the golden syrup, together with the sultanas and lemon halves. Turn the heat very low, put a lid on the saucepan, and simmer for 2 hours, stirring occasionally. About 15 minutes before serving, pick up the lemon halves with the kitchen tongs and squeeze them so that the juice goes into the curry (discard the lemon halves when this has been done). Serve with rice and accompaniments.

INDONESIAN CURRY

Accompaniments: With this curry serve the rice individually moulded for each person. Press the cooked rice into cups and then unmould immediately. (You can keep the rice hot by standing the cups in a covered shallow pan of gently boiling water before unmoulding it.) As many side dishes as you wish may be prepared, and should include prawn crisps, fried bananas, hot chutney and very small meat balls.

Coconut Milk: The liquid used in Indonesian curry is coconut milk, which is not the milk from the inside of this nut but an infusion of grated coconut and water. It is made by pouring hot water on to desiccated coconut, the quantities usually being 3 tablespoons of coconut to 1 cup of water. After the coconut has been soaking for 1 hour or more, strain the liquid through a muslin cloth and gently squeeze the residue through the cloth to extract the goodness and flavour. A lesser quantity of grated fresh coconut to the same amount of water may be used instead.

HOT CHICKEN CURRY

Substitute fish or another meat for the chicken in this recipe if you wish. This dish improves with keeping and should be made the day before it is to be eaten.

Dill Seed

- 1 small chicken, jointed and cut up
- 2 tablespoons groundnut oil
- 1 onion, chopped
- 2 cloves of garlic, chopped
- 2 tablespoons peanut butter
- 2 teaspoons salt
- 1 tablespoon flour
- 1 pint coconut milk (see the preceding recipe)

Spice Mixture

- 1 tablespoon chilli powder
- 1 dessertspoon ground cumin
- 1 dessertspoon turmeric
- 1 dessertspoon ground coriander
- 1 dessertspoon ground ginger
- 2 lemon or lime leaves

Warm the oil in a saucepan, and fry the onion and garlic in it until soft. Add the peanut butter and the salt. Mix the spices together in a small dish and add 2 or 3 tablespoons of them to the mixture in the saucepan. Add the flour. Stir and cook until well blended. Gradually pour in the coconut milk, stirring all the time. Add the chicken, then the lemon leaves, and simmer for 2 hours. Serve with rice and accompaniments.

Dill Seed

Dill (*Anethum graveolens*), one of the Umbelliferae, is an annual plant, a native of southern Europe. Many centuries ago it found its way, like numerous other herbs, to the colder parts of Europe, where it became an attractive and useful wayside 'weed'. Today it grows in countries all over the world. The name stems from the Norse word *dilla*, meaning to lull: dill water, a decoction made from the seeds, was given to babies to soothe them as early as Saxon times, just as it is today. Yellow-flowering dill, very like fennel in appearance, is grown for its fresh, fern-like leaves and for the aromatic buff-coloured seeds which give food added flavour and make it more easily assimilated. It is more than coincidence that dill is put with cucumbers in the making of dill pickles, for this vegetable has the reputation of being rather indigestible. It is also one of the most appropriate herbs to use in cole slaw and in steamed

Dill Seed

cabbage. If you do not care for caraway seed, dill seed may be substituted, for the flavour though similar is not as strong as that of caraway.

Sow the seed in the spring after frosts, where the plants are to remain, and thin out later, leaving a foot between each (the plants grow to a height of three feet and over). It is unwise to plant dill near fennel, for when you come to collect the seeds you will find that the mature plants are so similar in appearance and flavour that it will take time and close examination to sort them out satisfactorily. Dill is a more delicate plant in every way; the stalk is finer and the leaves have a more subtle flavour, reminiscent of caraway. Fennel is more like aniseed, and the seed-heads are smaller and not as heavy and full as dill. According to a charming American leaflet about herbs, dill and fennel seed were known as 'meetin' seed', having been given to children to eat during long Sunday sermons.

Dill seed is sprinkled on breads, rolls and apple pie; it is used in sauces for vegetables and fish; it goes into stews and soups; in the pot with those vegetables which need the minimum of water during cooking, such as shredded cabbage; it flavours pickles, chutney, potato salad and sauerkraut; and is often cooked with veal, pork and kidneys, and added to scrambled eggs and mashed potatoes. The pale-yellow flower-heads, too, are pretty enough to bring inside and arrange in a mixed bowl.

DILL PICKLES

When dill pickles are made at home in the correct way, they are so superior to the product sold in shops that it is almost like eating a completely different food.

The crispness of the cucumbers and the subtle flavours in the brine are the outstanding qualities of home-made dill pickles (or dill cucumbers as they are sometimes called). To achieve the desired crispness of the cucumber, there are certain simple but definite rules to be followed.

First of all it is important to grow your own cucumbers so that they may be freshly picked when they are only 4 or

Dill Seed

5 inches long, and put straight into the *coldest part of the refrigerator 24 hours* before putting them into the brine. This is the first step towards crispness.

With twelve little green cucumbers frosting under the ice trays, go into the garden and gather:

4 sprays of dill about 6 inches long	*1 spray of basil*
	1 sprig of tarragon
2 leaves from the grape vine	*1 tiny spike of rosemary*
	1 sage leaf

Then go back into the kitchen and place them in the bottom of a large saucepan, together with:

4 cloves of garlic	*4 to 6 crushed peppercorns*
½ dried bay leaf	*a few caraway seeds*
1 dry chilli	*¾ cup salt*

Add the cucumbers and cover with *boiling water*. This is the second step that ensures crisp cucumbers. Put the lid on the saucepan and leave to cool.

When cold pour the contents into a large screwtop jar, making sure the brine covers the cucumbers. Store for at least 2 weeks. When you begin to use them, first of all lift any mildew off the top. Keep the jar in the refrigerator once it is opened.

SCALLOPS WITH DILL

Roll 1 lb. of scallops in flour, egg and breadcrumbs, and fry in ¼ lb. of melted butter or margarine for a few minutes on either side. Put the scallops in a dish and keep hot. Stir 1 good tablespoon of flour into the fat, adding a little more if necessary, and blend well over medium heat. Pour 1 scant cup of stock or milk and 1 tablespoon sherry into the pan and stir until thick. Add 1 tablespoon of finely chopped dill, and pour the sauce over the scallops. Serve at once.

COLE SLAW WITH DILL

Cole slaw or cabbage salad is economical to make and tasty to eat in the summer either by itself with cold meat or served with other salads; it also goes equally as well with hot food in the winter.

Dill Seed

1 small firm cabbage	1 breakfast cup of mayonnaise
2 tablespoons chopped dill	1 chopped green apple

Trim and wash the cabbage, cut it into four and shred it as thinly as possible; the finer it is cut the better it is. Put the shredded cabbage into boiling salted water and boil for 5 minutes, then tip it into a colander and run cold water over it for a few minutes. Let the cabbage drain thoroughly, shaking it occasionally. When it is quite free of water put it into a bowl with the dill and apple, pour the dressing over and mix the salad well. It may be left overnight in the refrigerator with a plate over the top to prevent any odour from the cabbage affecting other food.

HOT SLAW

4 cups finely shredded cabbage	1 tablespoon sugar
2 eggs	2 tablespoons dill seed
¼ cup water	1 tablespoon butter or margarine
2 tablespoons lemon juice	salt and pepper

Break the eggs into a saucepan and whisk with a wire whisk. Add the water, lemon juice, sugar and dill seed, season with a little salt and pepper, and whisk well again. Place on a low flame, add the butter, and stir with a wooden spoon until the mixture thickens. Stir in the cabbage, coating thoroughly with the dressing. Serve hot.

DILL SAUCE

1½ cups white sauce	1 medium-sized dill cucumber, sliced
1 tablespoon sherry	2 teaspoons dill seed

To be eaten with any fried fish.

Mix the sherry into the hot white sauce, blend well, and add the cucumber and dill seed. Serve hot.

DILL-CHEESE DIP OR SPREAD

¼ lb. cream cheese	2 teaspoons lemon juice
2 tablespoons thin cream	1 tablespoon grated onion
2 teaspoons dill seed	salt and pepper

Blend the cheese and cream together, then add the rest of the ingredients, and mix well.

Fennel

Fennel is another native from Mediterranean countries, and also belongs to the Umbelliferae. Long ago it was taken to other lands by the Romans, and today it is widely grown in most parts of the world. The two best-known varieties are perennial, sweet fennel (*Foeniculum vulgare*) and the annual Florence or finocchio fennel (*F. vulgare dulce*). The former kind grows tall and feathery, and in early autumn its massed golden flowers foam along country roadsides; the leaves are not as tender and delicately flavoured as those of the annual fennel, which is a lower-growing type with bulbous, edible stems, a little like a squat celery in appearance. Fennel seed comes from both of these kinds, but if you are growing your own, it is suggested that Florence fennel is the wiser choice, since all parts of the plant may be used. Grow Florence fennel in a sunny position and give it plenty of moisture. When the base begins to swell, cultivate and feed the soil.

The broad white stems should be sliced thinly and added to green salads, or mixed with sliced asparagus and tossed in a French dressing with a dessertspoonful of finely chopped chervil (excellent with cold chicken). They are crisp and nutty, and the flavour bears a strong resemblance to that of aniseed, as in fact do all parts of this herb. The leaves are traditionally an accompaniment to fish, either in a sauce, or to be cooked with it. When the plant has finished flowering, and the heads are heavy with seed, collect and store the seeds. They go into breads and cakes, on top of rolls and fruit tarts, and in cheese mixtures and spreads. Fennel gives an aromatic taste to fish and meat dishes, especially pork, liver and kidneys; it goes into pickles and sauces, and is an ingredient in some curry blends.

Fennel is mentioned in the early Anglo-Saxon herbals; it was regarded as one of nine sacred herbs, and its properties

Fennel

were said to have great physical benefits and to guard against unseen evil. One of its ancient uses was for the restoration of eyesight; another use was as a decoction 'to make those more lean that are too fat'.

Chaucer mentions fennel:

> *Downe by a little path I fond*
> *Of mintes full and fennell greene.*

Shakespeare too knew fennel well:

> OPHELIA: There's fennel for you, and columbines; there's rue for you; and here's some for me; we may call it herb of grace o' Sundays.

Fennel is represented in Shakespeare's birthplace garden; the plant list is long and reads like poetry: amongst the medlars and mints grow bay trees, box and briar; columbine, cuckoo-buds, elder and fennel; savory, sedge, thyme and many more.

Longfellow describes tall, perennial fennel in 'The Goblet of Life':

> *Above the lowly plants it towers,*
> *The fennel, with its yellow flowers,*
> *And in an earlier age than ours*
> *Was gifted with the wondrous powers,*
>   *Lost vision to restore.*

COOKED FENNEL

Pull the fennel from the ground and cut away the leafy tops (put them in the refrigerator wrapped in tin foil for using some other time), wash well and cut into pieces. Simmer gently until tender. Drain. Make a white sauce and add the cooked fennel. Heat through and stir in a dessertspoon of chopped parsley before serving.

FENNEL CREAM SAUCE
(for fish)

1 cup cream
1 tablespoon lemon juice
1 teaspoon honey
2 tablespoons finely chopped fennel
salt and pepper

Fennel

Whip cream until thickened but not too fluffy, stir in the honey and lemon, blending well. Add fennel and seasoning last.

FENNEL-SEED SAUSAGE

A home-made sausage eaten cold is delicious and also nourishing, as well as being economical. With a good basic recipe, there can always be variations in the flavour and meat. For instance, 2 lb. of sausage meat could be substituted for 2 lb. of minced steak. The fennel seeds may be omitted. Garlic, onion, and parsley may all be added separately, or together. It is entirely a matter of taste. This recipe is simple, and is such a family favourite that it vanishes almost immediately.

2 lb. minced steak
2 eggs
4 cups soft breadcrumbs
2 level tablespoons of fennel seeds
1 chopped onion
salt and pepper

Put the meat, breadcrumbs, fennel seeds, onion, salt and pepper in a bowl, add the beaten eggs and mix well together. Have ready a clean floured cloth. Form the mixture into a sausage on the cloth, and roll the cloth well round, tying each end with string. Put into a large saucepan of boiling water, and boil for 2½ hours. Lift out carefully on to a plate, unfold the cloth and slip it away from the sausage. Roll the sausage in dry breadcrumbs and leave to cool.

KIDNEYS AND MUSHROOMS

6 sheep's kidneys
2 oz. butter
1 clove of garlic, chopped
1 onion, chopped
1 rounded tablespoon plain flour
1 teaspoon paprika
½ pint stock (may be made with soup cube)
½ lb. mushrooms
1 scant dessertspoon fennel seed
salt and pepper

Melt the butter in a heavy frying pan, and soften the garlic and onion in it. Skin the kidneys, slice them, and put them into the pan. Cook gently, turning them. Stir in the flour, allowing it to brown slightly, then add the paprika, stock, mushrooms and

Garlic

fennel seed. Stir until the sauce has thickened, adding salt and pepper to taste. Serve hot with buttered toast.

FENNEL-SEED POTATO CAKE

A new and tasty way with potatoes is always welcome. This dish is very little trouble to prepare. Peel and slice 1 lb. potatoes thinly, butter a baking dish and put in a layer of potatoes, 1 teaspoon fennel seed, and some salt and freshly ground pepper. Dot with butter. Repeat. Finish by pouring ¼ pint thin cream over the top. Bake in a moderate oven (gas 4, electric 350°F.) for about 1 hour. If becoming too crisp around the edges, cover with a piece of brown paper. Test with a fork: when soft in the centre, the potato cake is cooked. Serve hot.

FENNEL TEA

Boil ½ pint water with 1 teaspoon fennel seeds for 5 minutes. Strain.

Garlic

Garlic (*Allium sativum*) has a place in every store cupboard, for the discreet use of this pungent herb improves many dishes. The bulb is the part that is used. It is made up of separate sections called cloves, covered by a light skin, which is peeled before using.

Garlic was once known as a valuable medicinal herb, and today it is still highly regarded by many people for having a beneficial effect on the digestive system and for improving the complexion.

If you like garlic, it is a temptation to use it quite lavishly, and to eat it raw, perhaps finely sliced on bread with cheese. This is rather hard on other people for the effects stay for a long time! Unless you are contemplating a day or two of solitude, it might be wiser to follow Bottom's counsel in *A Midsummer Night's Dream* and 'eat no onions nor garlic, for we are to utter sweet breath'. A clove of garlic rubbed round a wooden salad bowl, or garlic butter spread on a hot French loaf, is usually sufficient when using it raw.

When cooked, especially for a long time, garlic imparts its fragrance to the dish, while not being in any way offensive to those who are prejudiced against it. It is astonishing how many cloves may be used in one dish, with the addition of shallots, without making it overwhelming, providing it is cooked long and slowly.

Garlic belongs to the same family as the shallot, onion, chives, leek and rocambole. Grow it in rich, friable soil, planting the cloves to a depth of 2 inches, and 6 inches apart, in late winter. Keep the bed weeded and watered. The bulbs may be lifted and stored the following summer or early autumn, the best of the cloves being kept on one side for planting again at the right time.

There are numerous ways of using garlic. Here are three suggestions that will be found particularly helpful.

1. When roasting lamb or mutton, especially if it seems to be a little tough, make one or two incisions in the raw meat with a knife and insert small cloves of garlic. It seems to act as a tenderizer as well as flavouring the meat deliciously.

2. Rub a small square of bread on both sides with garlic and place at the bottom of the salad bowl with the lettuce on top. By the time you come to toss it, the aroma will have penetrated the lettuce.

3. Chop 6 cloves of garlic very finely until it is almost pulp, then mash it into $\frac{1}{2}$ lb. softened butter. Spread on slices of hot crusty French bread and serve in a basket with any luncheon dish.

CASSEROLE SAUSAGES IN CIDER

8 *sausages*
2 *apples*
4 *shallots*
2 or 3 *cloves of garlic*
1 *cup of cider*
2 *tablespoons of flour*
sage and parsley
salt and pepper

Roll the sausages well in flour and fry them lightly all over in a little clear fat. Put them in a casserole dish with layers of sliced apple, cored but not peeled, finely chopped shallots (do not discard the green part; it is edible and adds colour), finely chopped garlic and some sage and parsley. Season with salt and pepper. Add a cup of cider. Cover and cook in a medium oven for 1 hour.

STUFFED STEAK ROLLS

1½ lb. round steak   1 cup of stock, water or red wine

Stuffing

3 oz. soft breadcrumbs
2 rashers of bacon cut into small pieces
2 cloves of finely chopped garlic
1 dessertspoon each of chopped onion, celery and parsley
1 tablespoon of melted butter

Cut the steak into strips. Combine the stuffing and spread on the strips. Roll up and secure with wooden toothpicks. Roll lightly in flour and brown in a little fat. Add the liquid, and simmer in a medium oven for 2 hours.

Scented-Leaved Geraniums

Scented geraniums are a valuable addition to the herb garden, not only because their leaves impart subtle depths of perfume to pot-pourri, but also because they may be used to flavour certain foods. All geranium leaves have a rather pungent quality. This is much more marked in some kinds than in others, and there are a number of varieties whose leaves are redolent of familiar scents which brings to mind the interesting fact that plant scents have their own tones and variations, just as in music and colour.

There seems to be an essential element which makes some plants smell of apples, lemons, roses and so on. The apple-scented geranium, *Pelargonium odoratissimum*, for instance, smells strongly of Granny Smith apples even when lightly brushed in passing. It is a delicate spreading plant, with round, green leaves and fragile, white flowers, valuable for borders or in the rockery.

Scented-Leaved Geraniums

The nutmeg-scented geranium, *P. fragrans*, at first glance is rather similar, but it is of more upright growth, and when the ruffled leaves are crushed the spicy scent reminds one of freshly ground nutmegs. The rose-scented geranium, from which the well-known oil of geranium is extracted, is said to be *P. capitatum*, although there is another variety known as attar-of-roses, or *P. graveolens*, which is thought by many to be the rose geranium, its leaves having much the same elusive perfume. The variety Lady Plymouth is also rose scented, and the leaves are variegated green and gold.

The lemon-scented geranium, *P. limonium*, has leaves smelling of lemons and something more, which is probably verbena, and this may be the reason why it is often called 'lemon-scented verbena'. The crisp leaves are long, very serrated and decorative, and the flowers, a delicate shade of pinky-mauve, are small and single. One or two leaves are often used to flavour jellies, custards, rice puddings and sponge cakes; when dried they give their warm yet lemony fragrance to pot-pourri, and the dried flowers, too, impart their fragrance and colour. The leaves of this variety are excellent for use in flower arrangements.

Some other varieties smelling of lemons are *P. asperium*, which has similar leaves to the lemon-scented, except that they are very sticky, and the decorative *P. crispum variegata*, which looks like a miniature cypress tree and whose lemon-scented leaves are small, curly and variegated.

Many people consider that *P. tomentosum* is the most fascinating variety of the scented-leaved geraniums. The peppermint-scented leaves are large and velvety, of a clear-green colour. There are recipes for using the leaves to make peppermint jelly, and if you wish to follow a Greek custom flavour apple jelly by putting them, as well as other sweet-scented geranium leaves (only two or three at a time), into the preserving pan during the last five minutes of cooking. Take them out before sealing the jelly in pots, but a fresh leaf may be put in for decoration and flavour.

In flower arrangements the peppermint-scented leaves lend contrast in texture and form against other leaves and as a soft

Scented-Leaved Geraniums

foil for flowers; red roses nestling against the tender green of these leaves are particularly enchanting. The plant itself is rampant and sprawling, and likes room to grow; the small white flowers, as is often the case with sweet-scented geraniums, are insignificant.

An interesting scented variety is the coconut-scented *P. enossularoides,* which has crimson flowers and leaves similar to the apple-scented geranium. Another is *P. abrotanifolium,* sometimes known as southernwood, the scent of the leaves being exactly like that of southernwood or lad's love.

Clorinda is sweetly named and lovely to look at with eucalyptus-scented leaves of brightish-green and single pelargonium-like flowers of rich cyclamen. *P. denticulatum* has very cut and fragile leaves, which are sticky and smell warm and spicy. It has mauve flowers. Fair Helen or Fair Ellen is an old favourite with large, pungent oak leaves and magenta flowers. Besides the ones mentioned here there are many more, an almost bewildering variety, and all a lesson in scent perception.

Last but not least in this chapter of geraniums is the little herb Robert, or Geranium Robert, as it is sometimes called. It is an annual with a delicate trailing habit, small round leaves and single deep pink flowers; today it makes a delightful herbaceous plant, but it was once valued in herbal therapy for its styptic qualities.

All the scented-leaved geraniums may be dried and used in pot-pourri except the sticky varieties. It is important to dry the peppermint-scented leaves carefully as they are inclined to retain moisture and to mildew. Spread them out on paper in warm, dry weather when there is no humidity in the air. Constance Spry suggests that scented geranium leaves can improve the flavour of a cake.

ATTAR-OF-ROSES SPONGE

4 *eggs*	*rose-geranium leaves*
6 *oz. sugar*	1 *level tablespoon butter*
5 *oz. self-raising flour*	4 *tablespoons hot water*
2 *level tablespoons cornflour*	*pinch salt*

Separate the egg-whites and beat until stiff, gradually add the sugar and beat until it is dissolved, then gently mix in the egg-yolks. Sift the flour, cornflour and salt 3 times, lightly fold it into the cake mixture, have the butter melted and the hot water ready, and fold in carefully. Grease and lightly flour two 8-inch cake tins, lay the rose-geranium leaves on the bottom of the tins and pour in the cake mixture. Bake in a fairly hot oven (gas 7, electric 400°F.) on the bottom shelf for 20 minutes. Turn out on a wire tray and leave to cool. The geranium leaves may be left on the bottom of the cake until ready for filling, allowing the flavour to penetrate. Fill the sponge with cream and sift a little icing sugar on the top. The perfume from the geranium leaves will linger, giving the cake a subtle fragrance.

LEMON-SCENTED BAKED CUSTARD

3 *eggs*	1 *medium-sized lemon-scented*
1 *pint milk*	*geranium leaf*
2 *tablespoons sugar*	*a little butter*

Break the eggs into a fireproof dish, add the sugar and beat together with a fork. Pour the milk gradually on the eggs, beating all the time. Dot with butter and place the geranium leaf in the centre of the custard. Put the dish in a pan containing about an inch of cold water and cook in a medium oven until the custard is set, about ¾ hour. The geranium leaf gently imparts its lemony aroma to the custard – a plain rice pudding may be flavoured in the same way.

PEPPERMINT JELLY

4 *lemons*	*green colouring or crème de menthe*
½ *lb. sugar*	*peppermint-scented geranium*
1 *pint very hot water*	*leaves*
3 *dessertspoons gelatine*	

Pick and wash a bunch of peppermint-scented geranium leaves, put them in a basin and bruise with a spoon. Squeeze the lemons and pour the juice on the geranium leaves, add the sugar. Cover the basin and leave for at least 2 hours. Strain the liquid through a sieve, pressing all moisture out of the leaves. Dissolve the gelatine in a little of the hot water, pour the rest

Ginger

of the water and dissolved gelatine into the peppermint-scented liquid. Add a tablespoon of crème de menthe if you wish, or a few drops of green colouring, and stir well. Pour the jelly into a dish and decorate the centre with a peppermint-scented geranium leaf. Leave to set.

BAKED APPLES WITH GERANIUM LEAVES

4 green cooking apples
1 tablespoon apple jelly
4 apple-scented geranium leaves
a little butter

Wash the apples, cut a little of the peel away from the top and core. Put a little butter into the hollows in the apples, add 1 teaspoon of apple jelly to each apple and top with an apple-scented geranium leaf. Stand the apples in a little water in a fireproof dish and bake in a medium to hot oven until just soft. Pour the liquid from the dish into a saucepan, add 1 tablespoon of sugar and boil for a few minutes, add a little red colouring and pour the syrup over the apples. Eat them hot with thick cream, and the geranium leaves, which become crisp, are edible too.

Ginger

Ginger (*Zingiber officinale*) is a native of tropical Asia, grown also in Africa, India, China and Jamaica. The perennial root is tuberous and creeping; after the plant has died down, the root is dried and then preserved in syrup, or it is crystallized or ground.

Ginger is an important ingredient in the blending of curry powder, and its rich, clean tang has been appreciated for hundreds of years in many different kinds of food. Whole pieces in syrup sealed in pretty blue and white or other attractively coloured patterned jars from the Orient have been a favourite of mine since childhood. In its crystallized, sugary form ginger makes a pungent sweetmeat, and small pieces added to the ingredients give added flavour to rich spice cakes.

Ginger

Green ginger is sometimes called for in recipes: this is usually available canned and preserved in liquid. Pieces of the whole root are used in marinades for teriyaki (a recipe for Beef Teriyaki is given below), in pickles and chutney, in Chinese food, and in some recipes for ginger beer and ginger wine. Ground ginger may nearly always be substituted for the whole root if necessary, and in this form it is used in ginger beer, ginger snaps, gingerbread, sauces, spice cakes, preserves and sweets, and to flavour certain meat and vegetable dishes.

Gingerbread men and other gingerbread fancies used to be sold at country fairs. Flora Thompson gives us a glimpse of highdays and holidays of the past in her *Lark Rise to Candleford*. Of one feast-day holiday she writes: 'The women made their houses very clean and neat for Feast Monday, and, with hollyhocks nodding in at the open windows and a sight of the clean, yellow stubble of the cleared fields beyond, and the hum of friendly talk and laughter within, the tea parties were very pleasant. At the beginning of the eighties the outside world remembered Fordlow Feast to the extent of sending one old woman with a gingerbread stall. On it were gingerbread babies with currants for eyes....'

BEEF TERIYAKI

The steak in this recipe may be replaced by pork, veal or chicken.

1½ lb. rump steak, cut into 2-inch squares
1 medium-sized tin pineapple rings, cut into quarters
1 small jar stuffed olives
red glacé cherries

Marinade

1 clove garlic, crushed
¼ cup soy sauce
1 teaspoon ground ginger
1 tablespoon sherry
juice from pineapple rings

Combine the ingredients for the marinade. Add the steak, leaving it to soak for 1 hour. Now thread alternately on 6-inch metal skewers the meat, pineapple pieces, olives, and cherries. Grill, turning frequently and basting with the marinade. Allow

2 or 3 skewers for each person. Serve with boiled rice and a green salad. Tomatoes can be used in place of the cherries.

For a barbecue, increase the quantities and thread on very long skewers, adding some or all of the following: mushrooms, small onions or pickled onions, capsicum slices, stoned prunes, thickly sliced dill cucumbers, gherkins, wedges of tomato and some stoned black olives. Rest the skewers over the coals, turning them until the food is cooked.

MANGO MOUSSE

The incomparable taste of mangoes is enhanced by the ginger in this sweet with the tropical fragrance.

2 large ripe mangoes or a 1-lb. tin
½ pint water
4 oz. sugar
1 teaspoon ground ginger
1 envelope gelatine (dissolved in ¼ cup hot water)
2 eggs, separated
½ pint cream, whipped

Simmer the water, sugar and ginger together for a few minutes. (If tinned mangoes are used the syrup from the tin may be substituted for the water and sugar.) Peel and slice the mangoes, add to the syrup, and poach until soft. Sieve them (syrup included) or put into a blender. Add the dissolved gelatine and return the mixture to the saucepan with the egg-yolks. Stir over low heat until smooth and thickened (do not boil). Remove from the stove, cool slightly, and fold in the whipped cream and the beaten egg-whites. Pour into a bowl or into individual dishes. Chill. Just before serving, cover the top with shredded coconut (for extra flavour and crispness brown the coconut beforehand in the oven).

Four medium to large peaches or a 1-lb. tin may be used if mangoes are not obtainable.

RED TOMATO RELISH

A quick, uncomplicated recipe to make when tomatoes are plentiful. The ground ginger and chilli powder give an invigorating flavour to this relish.

6 lb. ripe tomatoes
2 onions
2 teaspoons ground ginger
1 teaspoon ground mace

2 cloves of garlic	1 rounded dessertspoon chilli powder
1 lb. demerara sugar	
1 cup herb or cider vinegar	1 dessertspoon dried oregano
2 oz. salt	

Thickening
2 tablespoons plain flour and some vinegar

Pour some boiling water on to the tomatoes and leave for a few minutes. Drain the water off. Peel and chop the tomatoes. Peel and slice the onions and garlic. Put all ingredients except the thickening together into a saucepan and boil gently for 30 minutes. Blend the flour with enough vinegar to make a thin paste, pour into the mixture, and boil for a further 15 minutes, stirring all the time. Cool, then seal the relish in jars.

Juniper Berries

These are the fruit of a small, evergreen tree (*Juniperus communus*), native to Europe, northern parts of Africa, and Arctic regions. The berries do not ripen until the second or third year, when they are picked and dried. While the berries are ripening from green to silvery purple, new small cones are forming on the tree at the same time.

Not only does the resinous, sweetly sharp flavour of juniper berries give a delightful smell and taste to food, but an oil from the berries is used medicinally for the treatment of kidney and digestive complaints; the aromatic globes also provide the flavouring in the manufacture of gin.

In France, juniper berries are included in many stews, while in Germany they are considered an excellent addition to sauerkraut and cole slaw. These berries are almost essential with game dishes, such as duck, grouse, quail, hare, rabbit and venison; they are equally delicious in a stuffing for the domestic fowl, duck, goose or turkey. Six to nine berries are usually sufficient to give the desired flavour, and they should be crushed first with the back of a wooden spoon: this is easy to do because they are soft.

Juniper Berries

CHICKEN JUNIPER

This recipe allows 4 or 5 good servings. If you want enough for 6 to 8 people, cook 2 chickens and double the quantity of the ingredients.

Duck may be cooked in the same way, with sage substituted for the mixed herbs in the stuffing.

- a 2½- to 3-lb chicken, cleaned and ready to cook
- 2 oz. soft breadcrumbs
- 2 teaspoons mixed herbs
- 9 to 12 juniper berries
- salt and pepper
- a little grated lemon rind
- ½ pint white wine
- 2 carrots, thinly sliced
- 2 shallots, thinly sliced
- 1 tablespoon butter

Combine the breadcrumbs, mixed herbs, slightly crushed juniper berries, salt, pepper and lemon rind, and stuff the chicken. Spread the butter over the chicken and place it in a baking dish. Pour in the white wine and add the carrot and shallot. Cover the chicken with foil and bake in a moderate oven (gas 4-5, electric 375°F.) for about 1½ hours (lower the heat while cooking if necessary). To serve, lift the chicken on to a hot plate and pour the juices and vegetables over it. Buttery jacket-potatoes make a good accompaniment – they may be baked on a separate shelf in the oven at the same time. Pass round a green salad.

JUNIPER SAUERKRAUT

- one 16-oz. tin, or 1 pint, sauerkraut
- ½ pint stock
- 1 onion, chopped
- 1 clove of garlic, chopped
- 1 apple, chopped
- 2 oz. butter or margarine
- 1 cup yoghurt, sour cream, or thick cream
- 5 to 8 juniper berries, crushed
- 1 teaspoon celery seed

Soften the onion, garlic and apple in the butter over a low heat, add the crushed juniper berries and the sauerkraut, celery seed and stock. Simmer for a few minutes. Cover and put in a slow oven (gas 1, electric 300°F.) for 45 to 60 minutes. At the last stir in the yoghurt or cream. Serve hot with grilled pork, veal or sausages.

VEAL GRUYÈRE

2 lb. veal fillets	½ lb. Gruyère cheese, sliced
2 large onions, chopped	soft breadcrumbs
2 cloves of garlic, chopped	salt and pepper
4 oz. butter	12 juniper berries, crushed

Gently fry the onion and garlic in the butter until soft. Add the crushed juniper berries and a little salt and pepper. Transfer to a baking dish, lay the veal fillets on top of the onion, then add the slices of Gruyère cheese. Sprinkle thickly with breadcrumbs and bake in a moderate oven (gas 4, electric 350°F.) for 45 minutes.

Lavender

Nearly every garden has at least one lavender bush. It is not surprising that this beautifully scented small shrub has kept its popularity throughout the centuries, from long before the Christian era up to the present time.

There is no scent quite like lavender, each spray containing the warm, sweet smell of summer. Shakespeare, in *The Winter's Tale*, calls it 'hot lavender':

> *Here's flowers for you;*
> *Hot lavender, mints, savory, marjoram;*
> *The marigold, that goes to bed wi' the sun,*
> *And with him rises weeping. . . .*

Even on the bleakest winter's day, when a dried lavender flower or a lavender sachet is held and inhaled for a moment, a picture immediately forms of long, drowsy days, humming bees and a glowing tapestry of flowers in the garden.

Lavender is a *xerophyte*, which means that is especially adapted for living in dry conditions. The grey leaves indicate this quality, the greyness really being a mass of tiny white hairs, which are there to hold moisture within the plant. This is a planting guide to many grey-leaved plants: sage is another, as is the old-fashioned herbaceous border favourite lychnis, although if you were to snap any of these leaves in half you would find that they are green inside. Do not feel that rich soil will prevent a lavender bush from growing well. As long as it is well drained and not in clay soil, it will flourish. Working a little lime around the roots will benefit the plant under these conditions.

Pot-pourri is not complete without lavender, which retains its perfume long after the other flowers have faded, with the exception of rosemary. These two plants have strong, natural aromatic oils, which are known and valued by chemical firms and are extracted for commercial use.

The two common varieties are *Lavandula dentata,* and *L. vera.* The first is generally known as French lavender, and grows into a large bushy shrub with grey, serrated leaves and pale mauve blossoms. It likes a sunny position and light sandy soil, and is almost always in bloom, its main flush being in the winter. It is recommended for use as a hedge, and grows exceptionally well on a stone wall.

L. vera is the English lavender, and there are other varieties closely resembling it, known as *L. officinalis* and *L. spica.* It is a small-growing shrub, its smooth grey leaves are narrow and pointed, and the flowers which bloom in summer grow in long spikes of deep mauve. The scent of English lavender is incomparable, and for a low hedge it is ideal.

L. stoechas is also known as French lavender, and was once called by the quaint old name of sticadove. This dwarf variety is not often seen. It blooms in the spring and is worth growing for this reason and for its rich, purple flower-heads, similar in form to *L. dentata.* There is also a white flowering lavender, *L. officinalis alba,* which is rare and very sweet.

Any leaf or flower that comes from a lavender bush should never be wasted. When blooms that have been picked are spent, they may be tied in bunches to perfume drawers and linen cupboards, or added to the pot-pourri bowl, together with the aromatic leaves. Lavender should be pruned after flowering, to ensure a healthy well-shaped shrub. The prunings, of course, should not be wasted either. When lavender cuttings are put in sand, two thirds of each cutting should be

Lavender

stripped of its leaves; these leaves are gathered up and put straight into the large earthenware jar that contains pot-pourri.

Long ago lavender was used not only for making scented articles, but in confectionery, cooking and in medicine. There are delightful old recipes for lavender wine, lavender sugar, lavender water, lavender tea, the distilling of lavender for the volatile oil, as well as directions for making lavender fans, lavender bags and lavender quilted into caps. One charming idea that could be used today is to spear sweets and small pieces of fruit with spikes of English lavender.

AN AROMATIC BATH

This is a simplified version of an old recipe:

Boil for 5 minutes, in a sufficient quantity of water, one or all of the following plants: bay leaves, thyme, rosemary, marjoram, lavender, wormwood, pennyroyal, balm and eau-de-Cologne mint. Strain and add a little brandy. Shake the required quantity into a hot bath.

LAVENDER SUGAR

In the seventeenth century a favourite confectionery was Lavender Sugar, made by beating lavender flowers into three times their weight in sugar. If you put two or three lavender heads into the sugar canister they will scent the sugar beautifully.

LAVENDER WATER WITHOUT DISTILLATION
(from 'The Toilet of Flora' in *The Scented Garden*, by E. S. Rohde)

'If you would have speedily, without the trouble of distillation, a water impregnated with the flavour of Lavender, put two or three drops of Oil of Spike, and a lump of Sugar, into a pint of clear Water, or Spirit of Wine, and shake them well together in a glass phial, with a narrow neck. This Water, though not distilled, is very fragrant.'

LAVENDER VINEGAR

If you desire lavender vinegar to give a subtle fragrance to salads, steep lavender heads in 1 pint of white vinegar in a glass container on a sunny shelf for 2 weeks. Strain and use.

Although the little-known plant often called lavender cotton or French lavender (*Santolina chamae cyparissus*) does not belong to the lavender family at all, it may be included here to bring up the rear of the lavenders. With its fragrant foliage, resembling delicate grey coral, and round yellow flowers, it is a decorative and charming addition to any garden. It likes to grow in the same type of soil as the lavenders, light and well drained in a sunny position where it will attain a height of three feet with a spreading habit. Do not prune heavily.

Sprays of this herb were once laid in drawers to keep away moths, and oil for perfume from the plant is used industrially. The leaves and flowers are valuable in pot-pourri, adding colour as well as scent.

Mace and Nutmeg

Mace and nutmeg (*Myristica fragrans*) are grouped together because they both come from the same thirty-foot tropical tree, which grows in the Molucca Islands, Ceylon, Sumatra and Malaya. In some countries the species are different, and accordingly the shape and flavour of the fruit vary.

Imagine a section of the fruit cut in half: first there is the outer covering or shell, then the scarlet network or aril, which when dried is known as mace; within this lacy covering is the nutmeg.

The flavours of mace and nutmeg are very similar, mace being more piercingly aromatic. If mace is difficult to obtain, nutmeg may be substituted.

Nutmeg. Nutmeg usually comes to us ground, but the hard, dried seed may be kept in a small jar and grated when required. This spice has a pleasing and rather crisp, dry quality, and is often included in rich food. An egg flip or eggnog is not complete without a sprinkling of nutmeg on the top; besides having an agreeable flavour, nutmeg is supposed to have a soothing effect on the digestive system. It is interesting to read

Mace and Nutmeg

that its use in medicine is 'as a stimulant and carminative'. (A carminative is a medicine to cure colic or flatulence.) The flavour of nutmeg does not dominate when mixed with other herbs and spices.

Ground or freshly grated nutmeg flavours milk puddings, cakes, biscuits, soups, breads, oyster and fish dishes, pumpkin pie, cream sauces, some meat dishes and nearly all beverages made with milk.

Mace. The origin of mace has just been described. It may be obtained ground or whole. When whole it is known as a 'blade' of mace. The colour of dried mace is more golden than that of nutmeg, and the flavour is stronger, so a smaller quantity is required in cooking. Mace in a Sauce Suprême for fish is excellent. It is often called for in pickle and chutney recipes, in cheese dishes, to give character to creamed spinach, steamed young carrots and mashed potato. Grilled, buttered trout may be lightly sprinkled with salt, freshly ground pepper and a dusting of mace, all that this delicately flavoured fish needs.

FISH SUPRÊME

This dish may be made the day before and kept in the refrigerator; it should be removed an hour before it is ready to go in the oven.

Cover 2 lb. raw white fish with water, add a little salt and a bay leaf, and simmer until the fish is cooked. Drain, reserving the liquid. Flake the fish while it is still hot, removing all bones, and put into an ovenproof dish.

Make Sauce Suprême as follows: Melt $\frac{1}{4}$ lb. butter or margarine, blend in 2 oz. plain flour, and gradually add $1\frac{1}{2}$ pints fish stock, stirring constantly until it thickens. Combine 4 eggs, $\frac{1}{4}$ pint thick cream, 2 tablespoons white wine, $\frac{1}{2}$ teaspoon ground mace (or 1 teaspoon ground nutmeg) in a bowl, pour in some of the hot mixture, season with salt and pepper, mix well, then return all to the remaining contents of the saucepan. Stir gently over low heat for a moment only.

Pour the sauce over the fish, and top with soft white breadcrumbs which have been tossed in melted butter. Bake in a slow oven (gas 1, electric about 300°F.) until heated through. Serve hot with rice and chilled white wine.

SAVOURY WELSH RAREBIT

- 3 tablespoons butter or margarine
- 4 tablespoons plain flour
- 1 teaspoon mustard
- ½ pint milk
- 2 teaspoons beef extract (mixed into ¼ cup hot water)
- ½ lb. grated Cheddar cheese
- salt and pepper
- grated nutmeg

This cheese rarebit goes a long way.

Melt the butter, stir in the flour and mustard, slowly pour the milk in, then add the diluted beef extract. Add the cheese, season with salt and pepper, and cook, stirring until the mixture is smooth. Serve hot on buttered toast, topped with nutmeg.

AVOCADO SOUP

The most ambrosial soup I know. Ground or grated nutmeg sprinkled on each serving helps to minimize the richness without spoiling the bland texture.

- 1½ pints chicken broth (may be made with cubes)
- 2 large ripe avocado pears
- ½ pint cream
- extra cream
- ground nutmeg
- salt and pepper

Peel and stone the avocadoes, mash them, and put them into the chicken broth. Heat, then stir in ½ pint cream. Put the mixture through a sieve to remove any lumps, then return it to the saucepan, adding salt and pepper to taste. Bring slowly to simmering point without allowing it to boil. Serve hot with a dessertspoon of cream and a sprinkling of nutmeg in each bowl.

Marjoram

There are many different species of the valuable culinary herb marjoram, the most popular variety being knotted or sweet marjoram (*Origanum majorana*, one of the Labiatae). (For wild marjoram, see Oregano.)

Marjoram is a perennial and very easy to grow. Sow the seed in spring, or propagate by root division. It likes a sunny, well-drained position, and if cut back after flowering will grow into a healthy, shrubby plant about two feet high. The tight appearance of the milk-white flower-heads and buds gives knotted marjoram its popular name. When winter frosts have driven basil from the herb garden, marjoram comes into its own. It is difficult to choose between these two herbs for savoury flavour. Marjoram is more subtle, not giving its aroma as freely as basil. A light touch of the hand, or spray from the hose, will release the fragrance of basil, but you must pick a stalk of marjoram, when the soft and scented, greyish leaves will tempt you to nibble and enjoy their pungency.

Marjoram may be used in a number of ways, and it is wise to have more than one bush growing. Delicious brown-bread sandwiches are made with marjoram leaves spread thickly on a bed of cream cheese. Use the leaves in herb scones (a family favourite), in salads, omelettes and sauces, in vinegars, sweet bags and pot-pourri. There is also the customary bouquet of herbs for flavouring soups and stews, in which thyme, parsley, marjoram and a bay leaf are usually recommended.

Although marjoram was once used medicinally for a number of complaints – from digestive disorders to curing toothache – it was also highly valued as a 'strewing' herb on the floors of houses.

Marjoram is more pungent, perhaps, when dried than it is fresh. Although fresh herbs are probably superior, it is sometimes more convenient to use dried herbs, even when the former are available. When marjoram is just beginning to flower, cut some of it for drying, and proceed as described on page 18 for drying herbs.

OYSTERS BERCY

- 3 dozen oysters, drained
- 2 heaped tablespoons finely chopped shallots
- 2 oz. butter
- 1 cup white wine
- 1 dessertspoon lemon juice
- 3 teaspoons marjoram
- 1 scant tablespoon plain flour
- 1 cup thin cream
- salt and pepper
- ground nutmeg

Soften the shallots in butter without browning. Add the wine, lemon juice and marjoram, season with salt and pepper, and simmer over low heat until reduced a little. Mix the flour and cream together, add to the sauce and stir until thickened. Remove from heat, stir the oysters into the sauce, and spoon into ramekins or scallop shells. Sprinkle lightly with nutmeg, put into the oven, and heat through for 5 to 8 minutes. Serve hot with small squares of brown bread and butter.

Whitebait, scallops or sliced fish fillets may be used in place of oysters. Sauce Bercy may also be served over asparagus, sliced avocado pear, sautéed mushrooms or with delicately textured grilled meat.

COTTAGE PIE

This familiar dish is sometimes called Shepherd's Pie, another homely old name, indicating the popularity of the dish over the years. It consists of minced meat with a topping of mashed potato, and is always appetizing whether perfectly plain with only the addition of gravy and a little onion to the meat, or flavoured in a number of different ways. It is important to have the mashed potato crisp and golden. This recipe is for fresh meat, but it could be made with minced left-over meat and a cup of gravy, omitting the cup of liquid and the flour.

- 4 shallots
- 2 rashers bacon
- 1 clove garlic
- 1 lb. minced steak
- 1 tablespoon flour
- ½ pint stock or water
- 1 tablespoon marjoram leaves
- salt and pepper
- 1 lb. mashed potatoes
- oil

Marjoram

Wash and cut up the shallots, using as much of the green part as possible. Chop the garlic very finely. Cut the bacon into small pieces. Melt some oil in a large frying pan and cook these ingredients until soft. Add marjoram leaves and the minced steak. Press down with a fork, and brown all over, mixing the contents of the pan well together. Add the flour, cook a little longer, then pour in the liquid. Season. Turn into an ovenproof dish and top with creamy mashed potato. A tablespoon of nutty sesame seeds and pieces of butter spread over the potato before the dish goes into the oven are excellent. Bake in a medium oven for ¾ hour. If the top is not browned enough put under the grill for a few minutes before serving.

POTATO PIE

If you decide to serve one vegetable with a meal, potatoes with marjoram are quite substantial.

1 lb. potatoes
4 shallots
breadcrumbs
2 tablespoons marjoram leaves
¼ lb. butter
salt and pepper

Peel the potatoes and slice them thinly. Place in layers in a buttered pie-dish the potatoes, marjoram leaves, pieces of butter and finely sliced shallots. Top with buttered breadcrumbs and cook slowly in a medium oven, about 1 hour.

SUMMER VEGETABLE TART

Marjoram is used in a lightly scented seasoning for this tart, which may be eaten at luncheon or supper or taken on a picnic.

Rich Short-crust Pastry: Sift 6 oz. self-raising flour and a pinch of salt into a bowl, rub in ¼ lb. butter until the mixture is crumbly, add ¼ cup very cold water and a squeeze of lemon juice, and mix to a dry dough.

Filling: 1 cup cooked peas, 2 cooked carrots finely sliced, 1 cup cooked potatoes finely sliced, 2 tablespoons chopped shallots, 3 eggs, ½ cup cream, 3 teaspoons marjoram, some salt and pepper.

Roll the pastry out thinly and line a buttered 8-inch shallow pie-dish with it. Prick the pastry all over, and fill with the vegetables, arranging them attractively. Mix the eggs, cream, and marjoram together, seasoning with salt and pepper, and pour carefully over the vegetables. Bake in a moderate oven (gas 5, electric 375°F.) until set – about 30 minutes. Serve the tart warm or cold, decorated with a few fresh marjoram leaves.

BURNING STEAK

This way of preparing fillet steak is different, and fun to do. The flavour of the burnt brandy and the aromatic marjoram leaves sprinkled over the cooked steak make it a meal to be enjoyed.

4 pieces of fillet steak
butter
½ cup brandy

2 tablespoons finely chopped marjoram leaves
salt and pepper

Melt some butter in a heavy frying pan and put in the steaks. Let them sizzle, turn them over and cook a little longer. Pour the brandy over and set alight. When the flames have died down put the steaks on a hot dish. Pour the liquor from the pan over, dust with salt and freshly ground pepper, and top with the marjoram leaves.

VEAL IN APPLE JUICE

1½ lb. leg or shoulder of veal
1 15½-oz tin, or 2¼ cups, apple juice
2 tablespoons plain flour
3 teaspoons marjoram
2 teaspoons mustard seed

1 bay leaf
1 onion, finely chopped
1 clove of garlic, finely chopped
a few peppercorns
salt

Cut the veal into strips, roll them in flour and place half of them in an ovenproof dish. Sprinkle with half each of the marjoram, mustard seed, crumbled bay leaf, onion, garlic and peppercorns, with a little salt. Repeat, then pour the apple juice over. Cover, and bake in a moderate oven (gas 4, electric 350°F.) for 1 to 1½ hours.

HERB SCONES

While I was picking a bunch of parsley one day, a neighbour gave me this delicious recipe for using it in scones to put on top of a bubbling casserole or stew, half an hour before serving. In fact any savoury herb may be used that seems well suited to the dish it is accompanying. When roasting pork, mix rosemary leaves (cut up finely with the kitchen scissors) into the scones and bake on a tray in the oven. Served dry like this they are appropriate with a rich meat.

4 oz. self-raising flour
2 oz. butter
2 tablespoons chopped marjoram leaves
pinch salt and a little cold water

Sift the flour and salt. Rub in the butter. Add marjoram and enough cold water to make a stiff dough. Stir quickly and lightly with a knife and then pat out on the table with your hand. Cut into squares and use straight away, or wrap in tin foil and put in the refrigerator until needed.

MARJORAM VINEGAR

Fill a glass jar with marjoram leaves and pour the best wine vinegar over them. Cover and leave on a sunny shelf for 2 weeks. Strain and use.

Mint

There is a bed of mint to be found in nearly every garden. No wonder it has not vanished from our daily lives as so many other herbs have done; for besides being very hardy, the delicious, piercing quality of its scent has its own appeal.

Culpeper describes a formidable number of diseases in which preparations of this herb were used medicinally. It is mentioned in the New Testament and mints are described in early English plant lists.

Mint was valued for scenting baths and to 'strengthen the sinews' at the same time. It was also used as a strewing herb, in teas and in confectionery. Boiling a few sprigs of mint with new potatoes is believed to make them more digestible.

There are many varieties of mint, the best known being the curly-leaved spearmint (*Mentha spicata*) (this is the most

Mint

useful mint for drying). It is interesting to grow other kinds as well. Applemint (*M. rotundifolia*) which smells strongly of apples is recommended for mint sauce.

Eau-de-Cologne mint (*M. piperita citrata*), sometimes known as bergamot mint, has dark purplish leaves with an aroma definitely reminiscent of eau-de-Cologne. Put a sprig in the saucepan when cooking peas, and enjoy the scent that fills the kitchen, and at the same time delicately permeates the peas. This particular mint makes a refreshing tea on hot days.

The lower-growing peppermint or menthol (*M. piperita officinalis*) is the true Mitcham peppermint, and the oil from this plant is used commercially. A tisane made from menthol is highly esteemed for its beneficial effects when suffering from a cold.

Pennyroyal (*M. pulegium*), once valued for ridding rooms of fleas, is a pretty little edging or rockery plant with circlets of mauve flowers on miniature spires in spring. Its leaves, smelling and tasting of peppermint, are excellent when used liberally with new potatoes and butter.

The curly mint (*M. spicata crispata*), with its crinkly leaves, is used in mint sauce and is most attractive and tastes delicious when crystallized.

All the mints like fairly rich soil and plenty of water, and as they have rampant root systems, it is wise to give them room to grow. If space is limited, each variety may be confined in, say, a chimney pot buried up to the rim in the ground. Propagate by root division, preferably in winter or spring.

It has been found that leaves from a mint plant grown in the sun have a better flavour than those from a more lush-looking plant grown in the shade; but when cultivated in full sunlight, mint must be watered more frequently. It is well worth the small amount of extra work.

Mint may be dried on racks or in bunches hung in an airy place. The leaves should then be stripped from the stems and rubbed through a fine sieve. After having been treated in this way, 7 lb. of fresh mint is reduced to about 1 lb. The flavour is much stronger than that of fresh mint, of course, and only a small amount should be used at a time.

Mint

It is in the summer that mint is really appreciated for its fresh flavour and invigorating properties. In the making of fruit drinks it is invaluable, and some dried leaves mixed with package tea are refreshing on a very hot day.

Mint has many qualities, one of which is that it helps the digestion: peppermint tea is particularly good for this purpose, and it gives one a sense of relaxation and well-being at the same time. Mint has the reputation of repelling fleas, and it was used as a strewing herb in the Middle Ages. This herb with the warm, vital scent is used in numerous favourite recipes: in iced tea and fruit salads; with peas and new potatoes; as mint julep, mint jelly and mint sauce – to mention just a few. Recipes for mint teas are given on page 165.

Mint sauce for roast lamb is made in less than a minute by putting a dessertspoon of dried mint into a small jug with sugar, vinegar and hot water. For a change, sweeten with honey instead of sugar, and use lemon instead of vinegar, and remember there should always be lots of mint.

Tasty sandwiches are made with brown bread, cream cheese and finely chopped mint leaves.

Fry bananas lightly in butter with plenty of chopped-up mint to accompany crumbed cutlets.

A teaspoon or two of dried mint may be sprinkled on tomatoes just before they are grilled, fried or baked.

Shake a little dried or chopped fresh mint into scrambled egg, mashed potato or buttered vegetables before serving.

Mint is supposed to prevent milk from curdling. Eleanour Sinclair Rohde, in *A Garden of Herbs*, quotes this old recipe from *The Good Housewife's Handmaid*, 1588: 'Mintes put into milk, it neyther suffereth the same to curde, nor to become thick, insomuch that layed in curded milke, this would bring the same thinne againe.'

MINTED EGG TART

½ lb. cream cheese
6 eggs
3 tablespoons well-chopped mint
1 thinly sliced cucumber with the peel left on
short pastry (page 136)

Line a pie-dish with a thin layer of short pastry, spread with cream cheese or cottage cheese which has been mashed with some top milk or cream, and cover with the cucumber. Break the eggs on to this, season with salt and pepper and strew the top with mint, using spearmint or applemint. Bake in a moderate oven until the pastry is golden and the eggs set, about ½ hour. This is particularly delicious in hot weather, eaten cold for lunch, or to take on a picnic. A glass of icy apple cider and thin slices of cold ham or veal make excellent accompaniments.

FRENCH-STYLE PEAS

Shell 1½ lb. fresh young peas, or use a packet (8 to 12 oz.) of good-quality frozen peas. Wash the heart of a lettuce and arrange it in a saucepan, add the peas, 1 dessertspoon chopped spring onions, 2 teaspoons dried mint or 3 of fresh, a pinch each of salt and sugar and a few pieces of butter. Put the lid on the saucepan and place over a low heat. Shake the pan frequently at first; after a few minutes you will see that the peas are cooking in the moisture from the lettuce and the melted butter. Five to seven minutes is usually sufficient cooking time. Serve the peas and spring onions with the cooked lettuce, which is delicate and delicious.

MINT AND CHEESE DRESSING

To make this delicious dressing for baked potatoes, take 3 teaspoons of fresh or 2 teaspoons dried mint and 1 packet of cream cheese, and pound a small clove of garlic (and the fresh mint, if used). Mix thoroughly. Wash and dry some potatoes, rub them well with vegetable oil, and bake in a hot oven (gas 6–7, electric 400°F.) for 1 hour. Remove the potatoes from the oven, slit the tops with a knife and squeeze their sides slightly. Spoon the cheese dressing over them and serve hot.

MINT AND MARSHMALLOW CUSTARD

This simple milk pudding may be eaten either hot or cold. The marshmallows become caramelized, and the mint counteracts any tendency to over-sweetness.

With a fork beat together in an ovenproof dish 3 eggs and

1 tablespoon sugar. Gradually mix in 1 pint milk. Dust with 2 teaspoons dried mint or 3 of fresh and float about 24 marshmallows on top. Stand the dish in a shallow container of hot water, and place in a moderate oven (gas 4, electric 350°F.) to bake until set.

MINT JULEP

Wash a large bunch of mint (eau-de-Cologne mint is especially good) and put it in a basin. Bruise it and then add 1 cup of sugar, 1 tin of pineapple juice and the juice of 4 lemons. Cover and let it stand for some hours, then strain into a tall jug. Add 3 bottles of dry ginger ale, cubes of ice, thin slices of lemon and sprigs of mint. This has been a wonderful standby for luncheon on many occasions, and is preferred by many people to wine in the middle of the day.

MINT JELLY

1½ oz. gelatine
½ pint hot water
12 oz. sugar
1¼ pints wine vinegar
4 tablespoons chopped mint (*spearmint, applemint or curly mint*)
green colouring

Dissolve the sugar in the vinegar by bringing to the boil, and boil for 4 minutes. Dissolve gelatine in the hot water and add it with the mint and a pinch of salt to the vinegar. Bring it to the boil once more and remove immediately. Add a few drops of green colouring and allow to cool, stirring occasionally. When beginning to set put into small pots. Cover and keep in the refrigerator. Excellent with lamb, mutton, veal and pork as a change from mint sauce.

CRYSTALLIZED MINT LEAVES

Select the best leaves of curly mint, applemint or eau-de-Cologne mint. See that they are perfectly dry, and with a fine paint brush coat each one on both sides with a slightly beaten egg-white, then dust all over with castor sugar. Put on waxed paper in a warm oven to dry, leaving the door half open. Turn occasionally. When quite dry and glistening greenly, nibble one or two and see how delicious and pepperminty

PINEAPPLE COCKTAIL

1 *pineapple*
2 *tablespoons of finely chopped mint*
8 *oz. sugar*

Peel the pineapple. Stand it on a plate and slice downwards with a knife until the hard core is reached. Cut the pineapple pieces into cubes. Strain the juice into a saucepan with the sugar and mint and bring to the boil and simmer for a few minutes. Pour back on to the pineapple. Chill in the refrigerator and serve as an appetizer in individual dishes garnished with a fresh sprig of mint and a cherry.

The core and peel from the pineapple may be kept and simmered with sugar and water for about ¾ hour, then the liquid strained off and put in the refrigerator for drinks.

Mustard Seed

Mustard (*Brassica alba*) is an annual herb, native to Europe, Asia, and North Africa. It is interesting to note that there are no poisonous plants in the order Cruciferae (so called because the flower petals resemble a Greek cross). Mustard is only one of many well-known plants belonging to this family: among them are such familiar flowers, herbs, and vegetables as sweet alyssum, candytuft, wallflowers, woad, cress, horseradish, and cauliflower.

Tender young leaves of mustard and cress are old favourites together as salad and garnishing herbs. Mustard greens make an excellent salad on their own: as the larger leaves are quite hot they make an interesting contrast to certain foods. The leaves are an aid to health as well, and are still thought by many people to be a help in clearing the blood.

Mustard poultices and foot-baths, also still highly thought of, are ancient remedies for colds, fevers, and sciatica.

Mustard Seed

The mustard plant reaches 3 to 3½ feet in height and produces bright yellow flowers, followed by seed which may be dark red or, in the species *alba*, light yellow. In commerce both are blended together, sometimes with turmeric, to make powdered mustard. Another commercial form is a paste consisting of mustard powder, vinegar, sugar, and herbs; the ingredients added to the powder vary with each manufacturer. Whole mustard seed is extremely palatable, and may be used when the powder or paste will not do. One expects the seeds to be too hot to eat, but they are pleasantly nutty to bite on, the released flavour having only a mild tang of mustard.

Use mustard seed with discretion to begin with, increasing the amount as you become used to it. It goes into white sauce, mayonnaise, potato salad, cole slaw, steamed cabbage, herb butter (page 118), cheese dishes, and savoury spreads; it is used in fish, pork, and veal dishes, and is recommended for sprinkling over any salted meat while boiling; it is also a valuable addition to pickles and chutney. Lemon and Mustard Seed Chutney, the first recipe given below, is one of the most refreshing of preserves to eat with cold meat and curries, and to pass round at barbecues, the only drawback being that because of its popularity the whole batch disappears too quickly!

LEMON AND MUSTARD SEED CHUTNEY

4 medium-sized onions
5 big lemons
1 oz. salt
1 pint cider vinegar
1 teaspoon ground allspice
1 oz. mustard seed
1 lb. sugar
¼ lb. seedless raisins

Peel and slice the onions, cut up the lemons (discard pips), sprinkle with the salt, and leave for 12 hours. Add the remaining ingredients, bring to the boil, and simmer until tender (about 45 minutes). Spoon into jars and seal when cool.

FILLETS OF FISH MEUNIÈRE

Place ¼ lb. butter in the oven in a baking dish, and when it is melted and sizzling, put in the fillets (dipped in milk and coated with fine breadcrumbs), and sprinkle them with salt, pepper, and 2 teaspoons mustard seed. Bake for 40 to 60 minutes in a moderate oven (gas 4, electric 350°F.), basting occasionally. If they get too dry, add more butter. Serve hot, pouring any excess butter over the fish. A large translucent grape, peeled, pipped, and resting on each fish, is an attractive garnish.

HAM AND SWEET POTATO PIE

1½ *lb. ham*	2 *teaspoons mustard seed*
1 *lb. sweet potatoes*	2 *tablespoons brown sugar*
1 *large onion*	*a little butter*
½ *pint onion soup*	*salt and pepper*

Slice the ham, cut it into pieces, and put it into an ovenproof dish. Peel the sweet potatoes and the onion, slice thinly, and put in layers over the ham, sprinkling each layer with mustard seed, salt, and pepper. Pour in the onion soup. Sprinkle the top with brown sugar, dot with butter, cover, and bake in a moderate oven (gas 4, electric 350°F.) for about 1 hour.

The ham may be replaced with cold corned beef, or with cold cooked salted mutton.

Nutmeg

See Mace, page 95.

Oregano

A herb from the Labiatae family, and one highly regarded in Mediterranean cooking, is oregano (*Origanum vulgare*). It is one of the marjorams, but its leaves are far more pungent and hot than the sweet marjoram so it should be used more sparingly. The scent varies according to soil and climate.

The name *Origanum* comes from Greek words meaning 'joy of the mountains', which is very suitable because it

Oregano

grows in such a lively way, the bees clustering round the small white flowers when they appear, and the leaves seeming to absorb every ray of sunshine and clean, fresh air.

The plant has some resemblance to marjoram, the leaves being smaller and rougher; it has a creeping root system and a rather sprawling habit. Oregano likes to grow in light, well-drained soil in a sunny position. Seed may be sown in the spring, or the roots may be divided in the autumn, winter or spring. A plant, cherished carefully, will multiply to grand proportions. It is not wise to nibble oregano leaves indiscriminately for the powerful flavour is quite astonishing.

Here are some suggestions for the use of the herb.

1. Oregano should be dried when in flower for the full benefit of the aroma; stalks may be picked as they flower, hung up to dry, and then used.

2. For a tasty grilled steak, rub it first with a cut clove of garlic, and then brush melted butter on to the steak with a dried branch of oregano. Some of the leaves and tiny flowers adhere to the meat. Grill, then turn the steak and repeat the process.

3. Rub dried oregano leaves, or put them, freshly chopped, on top of tomatoes when baking, grilling or frying them.

4. Serve boiled spaghetti with a sauce mixed into it made from thinly sliced cloves of garlic, fried in oil until soft, peeled tomatoes, and oregano to taste. Top with grated Parmesan cheese.

STEAK KEBABS

Allowing ½ lb. meat for each person, cut fairly thick grilling steak into bite-sized cubes. Put the cubes on to skewers alternately with pieces of tomato, bacon, pineapple and pickled onions. Season with salt, pepper and dried oregano. Grill. These kebabs are ideal for a barbecue meal, and may be eaten with crisp bread rolls or a long French loaf, flavoured with garlic.

PIZZA PIE

When preparing pizza pie it is worth the trouble to make

Oregano

the bread dough with yeast in the traditional way for a dish loses its personality if made with short cuts. The rich smell of the yeast, the smooth, elastic softness of the dough beneath the fingers, and watching it rise in a warm place all give such satisfaction that, if only there were more time, making one's own bread would be a pleasurable and not difficult housewifely task. Once I had enough dough left over from the pie to make a miniature loaf for the youngest member of the family – a wonderfully risen round loaf with a beige top which looked exactly like the illustrations in children's storybooks!

Bread Dough
- ¼ lb. plain flour
- ⅛ pint warm milk and water mixed
- ¼ oz. yeast
- ¼ teaspoon salt

Filling
- 4 peeled and cut tomatoes
- 1 tin anchovy fillets
- 4 oz. thinly sliced cheese
- 1 dessertspoon fresh finely chopped oregano
- pepper and olive oil

Sift the flour and salt into a warm basin. Make a well in the centre and pour in the yeast which has been dissolved in a little of the warm milk and water. Fold the flour over the yeast with the fingers and keep folding it over until blended. Sprinkle a little flour over and round the dough, put a small blanket over the basin and leave in a warm place for the dough to rise (about 2 hours). The temperature should not be too hot or it will kill the yeast – 85 degrees is a good temperature and this may be achieved with a gas or electric oven with careful watching. (A wood or coke stove is ideal for the making of bread dough of course, for the basin may be left where the warmth will reach it.) When ready take the warm basin and stand it for a few minutes where the dough will be kneaded to avoid any sharp drop in temperature. Take out the dough, sprinkle a little flour on the table and knead gently with the fingers until it reaches the right consistency. This is felt immediately by a subtle change in the dough – it becomes light and elastic. Roll it out very thinly in two discs, place one on the bottom of a lightly oiled ovenproof dish, spread with the tomatoes, season with pepper, lay the anchovies on the tomatoes, then the cheese, and sprinkle the oregano on top. Pour 1 dessertspoon of oil over all and then place the other disc on top just sealing the edges of the pie together with the fingers. Put in a hot oven (gas 8, electric 450°F.) for 20 minutes and eat it warm. It makes an excellent luncheon dish accompanied with a French salad in the winter for four people.

SPAGHETTI BOLOGNESE

1 lb. minced steak	2 oz. olive oil or butter
1 clove of garlic, finely chopped	1 onion, peeled and chopped
½ pint tomato purée or 1 lb. fresh, peeled tomatoes	½ pint stock (may be made with a beef cube)
salt and pepper	3 teaspoons oregano
½ lb. spaghetti	

Garnish

1 tomato, sliced	1 capsicum, sliced
1 cup finely grated cheese	2 rashers rindless bacon
2 teaspoons parsley	

Heat the oil or butter in a heavy saucepan, and fry the meat, garlic, and onion until brown. Add the tomato purée or the fresh tomatoes, and the stock, salt, pepper, and oregano. Cover, and simmer gently for 30 minutes.

In the meantime cook the spaghetti in plenty of boiling, salted water until it is just soft (about 15–20 minutes), moving it occasionally with a fork so that the strands do not stick. Place it in a colander to drain, then pour hot water through it.

Take a greased casserole dish, put a layer of meat and sauce in the bottom, then half the spaghetti, another layer of meat and sauce, and finish with the rest of the spaghetti. To garnish, place the sliced tomato and capsicum over the top, sprinkle with the cheese, then the bacon (which has been cut into several pieces, each piece rolled up neatly and secured with a toothpick). Bake in a moderate oven (gas 4, electric 350°F.) until the cheese and bacon are cooked. Sprinkle the parsley over the top and bring the dish to the table.

OLIVES OREGANO

When black or green olives are steeped in a marinade of oil, herbs, and spices they acquire an added flavour and a mellow smoothness. Drain the olives for a short time before using them.

Prick 1 lb. olives with a silver fork and put them in a screw-top jar, add 1 cup vegetable oil, 1 teaspoon thyme, 1 teaspoon crushed peppercorns, and 3 teaspoons oregano. Top up with oil if necessary, cover, shake well and put into the refrigerator. Leave for at least 2 days, and use as required. Spear on wooden picks, or stone the olives and serve on vine leaves for lunch with black bread, two or three cheeses, and a light red wine. Especially delicious if eaten out of doors in the sunshine.

QUICHE LORRAINE

Line a buttered pie-dish with short-crust pastry (page 100). Prick all over. Remove the rind from ½ lb. bacon, cut into squares, and fry or grill until crisp. Place thin slices of Cheddar cheese on the pastry, then half the bacon and 1 or 2 teaspoons oregano. Repeat once more. Make a rich custard with ½ pint cream and 2 eggs, season with salt and pepper, and pour it over the cheese. Bake in a moderate oven (gas 5, electric 375 °F.) for 30 minutes or until cooked. When cool, strew the top with stoned black olives.

Paprika

Paprika (*Capsicum annuum*) comes from a red, sweet pepper that is native to Central America and cultivated today in different parts of Europe and the United States. It is dried, ground and sometimes blended with other peppers of the same family that differ in degrees of pungency. The best paprika is now said to come from Hungary.

The colour of paprika should be a rich, bright red, and the aroma warm and sweet. A splendid spice to use for flavouring, it is quite often regarded as a garnish only. Paprika gives Hungarian goulash its characteristic colour and taste; it is also valuable as a flavouring for delicately textured food such as crab, chicken, cream sauces, eggs, and cheese dishes. It may be mixed into rice dishes and shaken on to split, baked potatoes, hors-d'œuvre, casseroles, or salads.

HUNGARIAN VEAL GOULASH

2 *lb. veal steak*	1 *bay leaf*
2 *onions, sliced*	1 *dessertspoon lemon juice*
1 *tablespoon fat*	1 *cup cream*
1 *tablespoon paprika*	1 *tablespoon plain flour*
½ *pint stock (may be made with a beef cube)*	*salt and pepper*

Cut the veal into 2-inch cubes. Soften the onion in the fat, add the meat, and brown all over. Add the paprika, and salt and pepper to taste, and cook a little longer. Add the stock, put in the bay leaf, cover the saucepan, and simmer for 1 hour, stirring occasionally. (Add a little more liquid if becoming too dry.) Pour the lemon juice into the cream, blend in the flour, add to the veal, and stir until thickened. Serve hot with poppy-seed noodles (page 121).

WALDORF SALAD

Paprika gives sparkle and relish to this salad, which is crisp with celery, apples, and nuts, glistens with orange cubes, and is folded together with a creamy sauce. It makes a pleasant change from a tossed green salad to serve with a main course.

1 *crisp eating apple, chopped*	1 *cup diced celery*
1 *large sweet orange, peeled and chopped*	1 *packet shelled, halved walnuts* *paprika*

Sauce

1 *cup cream*	1 *tablespoon lemon juice*
1 *tablespoon sugar*	1 *teaspoon dry mustard*
salt and pepper	

To make the sauce, stir the lemon juice, sugar, and mustard, with a little salt and pepper, into the cream, and beat till thick. Mix together the apple, celery, orange, and nuts and pour the sauce over. Toss well, then chill in the refrigerator. When ready to serve, turn on to a bed of lettuce, or on to leaves of fresh herbs, and sprinkle rosily with the paprika.

TEN-MINUTE CRAB PAPRIKA

This is an excellent entrée and makes a pleasant snack for a late supper.

Open a 6½-oz. tin of crab and flake it, removing all the sharp pieces. Have ready 1 pint of rich white sauce. Heat (do not boil), stirring in an egg which has been beaten with 1 dessertspoon paprika. In a separate saucepan warm 2 tablespoons brandy, set alight and carefully add to the sauce. Stir well, then add the crab. Pour into a buttered ovenproof dish or buttered scallop-shells, and top with breadcrumbs which have been tossed in melted butter. Brown in the oven. Serve with thin slices of lemon and very small squares of brown bread and butter.

Parsley

A bed of parsley is almost indispensable, and it is looked on in much the same way as mint – a herb that we take for granted. It has been known all over the world for so many centuries that its origins are obscure, but it is thought to have come first from Sardinia.

There are many varieties of parsley, the best known being curled parsley (*Petroselinum crispum*), fern-leaved parsley (*P. crispum filicinum*), and 'Italian' parsley (*P. crispum neapolitanum*).

There have been more legends and superstitions about parsley than about any other herb, and many have come down to the present day. One belief is that if the seeds are sown on Good Friday they will bring happiness and good fortune; another that if parsley is planted around the onion bed it will keep away the onion fly; and another that if parsley is thrown into a fish pond, it will cure sick fish. There is probably a lot of truth in many of these old beliefs.

Parsley has been a valued medicinal herb extolled by writers since ancient times. Culpeper, quite a latter-day enthusiast comparatively, lists several different varieties, and has written nearly three pages on its virtues in treating all manner of diseases, particularly kidney and liver complaints. He also says it is a good salad herb.

In *The Truth About Herbs* Mrs C. F. Leyel writes: 'Parsley juice is rich in vitamin C and carotene and in most of the valuable organic salts. It is a useful general tonic, and acts specifically as a tonic for the kidneys.'

An old saying that parsley seed goes six times to the Devil and back before germinating reveals how slow it is in this respect! When preparing to put in the seeds in the spring or autumn they may be soaked in water for twelve hours before planting, to hasten germination.

Parsley is a biennial, although it may be kept as a perennial if the flower stalks are cut when they appear. If it is in the right position, moist and sheltered with some sun during the day, and in fairly rich soil, some of the plants could be allowed to go to seed, when they will self-sow with no trouble. To make the most of your plants, always pick from the outside, allowing the new leaves to develop from the middle.

Parsley is best fresh, but it can be used dried. Spread sprigs on racks, or hang them in bunches in a warm, airy room. It may also be dried quickly in a warm (*not* hot) oven. When crisp, rub through a sieve and seal in airtight containers. Use it for sprinkling on top of soups, for putting in mashed potato, all egg dishes, and in dumplings for a casserole or stew. Use it in sauces, mayonnaise and for parsley butter to accompany grills. Cut a lemon into wedges and dip the tops in dried parsley for an appetising garnish.

Today, as a culinary herb, parsley fulfils many requirements. It is excellent for garnishing, and adding, in a chopped-up form, to white sauce, scrambled egg and mashed potatoes. Many people do not know how rich in vitamins it is. When green vegetables are scarce, a tablespoonful of chopped parsley on each plate will help to make up the deficiency. Fried parsley with fish is really delicious. Parsley jelly and parsley ice are two excellent ways of using this herb.

Parsley

NOODLES AND MUSHROOMS

- 1 lb. noodles, any shape
- ⅛ teacup oil
- 2 tomatoes, peeled and chopped
- 3 cloves of garlic, finely cut up
- 2 tablespoons chopped capsicum
- 1 onion, chopped
- 1 lb. mushrooms, peeled and sliced
- ½ lb. bacon, grilled or fried, cut into pieces
- 2 dessertspoons fresh or 1 dessertspoon dried parsley
- salt and pepper
- grated Parmesan cheese

Heat the oil in a heavy saucepan and add the tomato, onion, garlic, capsicum, and mushrooms. Cook gently for 10 to 15 minutes, then add the bacon and parsley, with salt and pepper to taste. While preparing the mushroom mixture, have the noodles cooking in a quantity of boiling salted water, stirring them occasionally to prevent sticking. When soft, drain them well. Put into a warmed dish, cover with the hot mushroom mixture, and sprinkle generously with grated Parmesan cheese.

LAMB HARICOT

Have a leg of lamb cut right through into circles by the butcher. The meat is trimmed of fat and put into a large casserole with chopped onions, garlic, and tomatoes, a seasoning of salt, a few peppercorns, and a little stock. Bake with the lid on in a slow oven (gas ½–1, electric 250–300°F.) for 3 hours. Twenty minutes before serving, add 2 cups of cooked haricot beans. Finally, strew chopped parsley liberally over it.

PARSLEY JELLY

Wash a big bunch of parsley (about 50 stalks). Put in a saucepan with enough water to cover, add the peel from a lemon and boil for about 1 hour. Strain the liquid into a basin and add the juice of 3 lemons. Measure, allowing a cup of sugar to every cup of liquid. Boil again until it begins to set. Drop in a little green colouring to improve the appearance. Put in jars, seal down and keep in a cool larder or refrigerator and eat it with chicken or fish.

Parsley

PARSLEY BUTTER (GREEN BUTTER)

For grills, fish, and baked jacket potatoes. Other herb butters may be made in the same way.

Soften ¼ lb. butter with a fork and work into it a few drops of lemon juice and 3 teaspoons fresh or 2 teaspoons dried parsley. Spread on a saucer and place in the refrigerator to harden. Cut into cubes and put them on a dish to be handed round at the table, or place cubes on the food just before serving it.

FRIED PARSLEY

It is better not to wash the parsley, but if you do make sure it is absolutely dry before using. Break it up into sprigs and melt some butter in a frying pan. When the butter is hot and sizzling, but not black, put the sprigs in and let them fry quickly and crisply for about ½ minute or a little longer. Serve at once. The parsley should still be green, and not brown. Simple as this may seem, it takes a little practice which is well worth while.

PARSLEY ICE

1 *lemon*	2 *tablespoons finely chopped*
½ *pint water*	*parsley*
4 *oz. sugar*	1 *tablespoon dry sherry*
1 *stiffly beaten egg-white*	1 *tablespoon green colouring*

A water ice is sometimes eaten with the meat course. In hot weather it is particularly refreshing. Put the juice and finely grated rind of the lemon in a saucepan with the sugar and water. Bring to the boil and stir in the parsley. Simmer for 5 minutes. Cool, add the sherry and green colouring. Put in an ice tray and freeze. When crystals start to form take out and mix into the beaten egg-white. Return to the refrigerator to harden. It looks tempting when turned out on to a dish embedded in ice.

Pepper

Black pepper (*Piper nigrum*) and white pepper are both produced from the same climbing vine, which is native to the East Indies and cultivated in India, Sumatra, and Java. Pepper has been a valued spice for many hundreds of years; in the Middle Ages it was prized nearly as highly as gold and silver.

For black pepper, the berries are first picked from the vine, and then dried, when they become dark in colour, wrinkled, and very hot.

For white pepper, which is the same fruit, the dark outer husk is removed, leaving the smooth, parchment-coloured core, sharper in flavour than black pepper.

Both black pepper and white pepper come in several forms: ground to a powder, left whole, or sometimes coarsely ground and mixed with sweet red pepper, sugar, and spices to make a delicious seasoned pepper. It is interesting to make your own mixture: over a small dish grind black and white pepper together in a mill, into the powder put a little sugar, ground cinnamon, paprika, and a pinch of ginger. Use this as a garnish as well as for flavouring.

Whole pepper, or peppercorns, are becoming increasingly popular: they may be poured into a mill and freshly ground over food while it is being prepared, and the mill may be passed round at table as well. The flavour of newly ground pepper is more aromatic. It is a matter of taste whether black or white pepper is used for this purpose; sometimes a mixture of the two is preferred.

A few whole peppercorns should be dropped into soups, stews, and casseroles, or when boiling salted pork, mutton, or beef. They are used too when making pickles, spice vinegars, and sauces.

SAUSAGES AND LENTILS

2 lb. beef sausages	½ teaspoon peppercorns
2 medium-sized onions	2 tablespoons red lentils
1 clove of garlic	salt
3 cloves	plain flour
1 bay leaf	

Roll the sausages in plain flour, and peel and slice the onions and garlic. Put the ingredients in layers in an ovenproof dish and cover with water. With the lid on, bake in a slow oven (gas ½–1, electric 275–300°F.) for 2½ hours.

PICKLED ONIONS

One year a crop of white onions failed and we were given a quantity of pearly little vegetables that were too small to send to market. When pickled they were crisp and spicy. Here is the way to pickle them: Peel 1 quart of small white onions, strew 1 oz. salt over them, and leave overnight. Next day, boil 1 quart of cider vinegar with 1 dessertspoon each of black peppercorns and whole cloves for 10 minutes. Wash the salt off the onions, shake dry in a colander, and add to the vinegar. Boil for 5 minutes. Remove the onions and pack into small jars or a large pickle jar, then pour the vinegar on to them. Seal the jars when the contents are cold.

SPICED VINEGAR

Empty 1 bottle of white wine or cider vinegar into a saucepan. Add 1 teaspoon each of peppercorns, whole cloves, ground ginger, and celery seed, also 1 cinnamon stick, 1 dried chilli, and 1 dessertspoon sugar. Bring to the boil and simmer for 3 minutes. Cool and bottle without straining.

Poppy Seed

The slate-blue poppy seed used for cooking is produced from an annual poppy (*Papaver rhoeas*) that is native to Asia and

Poppy Seed

came centuries ago to Europe, where it grows wild in great abundance. These attractive plants are often seen in herbaceous borders with other old-fashioned herbs and flowers, and most of us are familiar with the many colourful varieties, both annual and perennial, which have been evolved for decorative garden displays.

Poppy seed is free of narcotic content, and so is the valuable oil extracted from the seed: opium is obtained from the unripe heads of the poppy *Papaver somniferum*. Morphine is a valuable product of opium. Of poppy's other medicinal virtues, Florence Ranson in *British Herbs* says: 'Poppy-heads have long been a rural remedy for toothache, neuralgia and other nervous pains, and once it was common to see bunches of the dried heads hanging in chemists' shops.' An infusion known as 'the soporific sponge', made from poppy, mandrake, hemlock, and ivy, and poured over a sponge to be held under the nostrils, was highly regarded in the Middle Ages as an anaesthetic.

Poppy seed is used extensively in European and in Eastern cooking. The tiny grains are a natural source of minerals, and are so pleasant to use in food that a jarful in the kitchen is almost indispensable. The seed may be used whole or ground. When ground it is combined with eggs, mixed candied fruit, sugar, and spice to make a nourishing fat-free and flour-free cake; a rich filling of ground poppy seed and other ingredients is made for strudels and ring cakes.

Whole poppy seed has a vast number of uses; it is sprinkled on breads, rolls, cakes, pies, mashed potato, and whipped cream; it is excellent in white sauce for vegetables, and in honey dressing for fruit; it is mixed with cooked noodles and butter, or with macaroni.

POPPY-SEED NOODLES

To accompany grills, casseroles, rissoles, goulash, stews, or meat loaf.

Put a quantity of water into a large saucepan with a pinch of salt and bring to the boil. Empty a packet of noodles into the saucepan. Continue boiling for about 15 minutes, or until the noodles are soft, stirring occasionally to prevent them sticking together. Drain in a colander, running cold water over them. Shake the noodles well and stand them on one side. Rinse and dry the saucepan, put 1 dessertspoon butter in and return it to the stove. Add the well-drained noodles and 1 tablespoon poppy seed. Re-heat, mixing well together. Serve immediately.

CONTINENTAL POPPY-SEED CAKE

1½ cups poppy seed
6 eggs, separated
1 cup sugar
½ cup mixed candied fruit-peel
1 teaspoon allspice
whipped cream

Grind the poppy seed in a grinder or electric blender, or have it ground at a delicatessen. The seeds may sometimes be bought already ground. Beat the egg-yolks until thick, and while still beating gradually add the sugar. Stir in the mixed peel, allspice, and ground poppy seed. Beat the egg-whites until stiff but not dry, and fold carefully and thoroughly into the poppy-seed mixture. Have ready a buttered and lightly floured spring-form cake tin, and pour in the cake mixture. Put it into a pre-heated slow to moderate oven (gas 3, electric 325°F.) and bake for about 50 minutes. Allow the cake to cool in the tin, then carefully remove the spring form. Spread the top of the cake with whipped cream before serving.

ALEXANDRA'S FRUIT AND POPPY-SEED PUDDING, COUNTRY STYLE

6 oz. self-raising flour
4 oz. sugar
a lump of butter
milk
1 tablespoon poppy seed
1 cup mixed candied fruit-peel

A good neighbour, Alexandra, once baked and gave me this pudding when we were very busy. It was popular with every member of the family.

Rub the butter into the flour and sugar, and add enough milk to allow the mixture to be spread into a buttered ovenproof dish. Cover with the fruit-peel and poppy seed, pressing well down, then sprinkle with a little sugar. Bake in a moderate oven (gas 5, electric 375°F.). Eat hot or cold with cream.

Rosemary

Rosemary (*Rosmarinus officinalis*), or 'dew of the sea', is an aromatic shrub which flourishes best and has more flavour when grown near the sea.

It was known to the Saxons and is referred to in one of the earliest herbals, the Saxon 'Leech Book of Bald'. It was greatly favoured too in Tudor days, not only for its appearance, but also for its usefulness in medicine and cooking. Shakespeare refers to it several times, Spenser called it 'cheerful rosemarie', and Sir Thomas More says 'I lette it run all over my garden walls'. It does look effective against brick or stone, and the low-growing variety, R. *prostratus*, is beautiful hanging in blue-flowered festoons over grey stones. The wood of rosemary was used to make lutes and carpenter's rules.

There are perhaps more legends wrapped around this freshly scented herb than any other. They are nearly all mystical or sacred. The French believed that the flowers rekindled lost energy, and they sometimes burnt branches of the bush for incense. It was also supposed to ward off black magic; it figured prominently on gay occasions such as weddings and banquets; and sprigs of rosemary to this day symbolize remembrance and friendship. In Australia a sprig is worn for remembrance on Anzac Day.

There is the holy legend that during the flight into Egypt, the Virgin Mary threw her robe over a rosemary bush while she rested beside it. For ever afterwards the flowers which were previously white turned blue.

A picture called 'The Legend of Rosemary', by Margaret W. Tarrant, shows Christ sitting on the ground while his Mother spreads his garments to dry on a rosemary bush. It is said this is the reason why the plant is so fragrant and 'That bush forthgives the faint, rare, sacred sweet of Him' (John Oxenham).

These and other sacred legends were probably the reasons

Rosemary

why it was believed that carrying a sprig of rosemary was proof against all evil, and that it should be carried by brides, as well as decorating churches on festive occasions.

The bracing and tonic effect of the leaves has always been valued. In *A Garden of Herbs* Eleanour Sinclair Rohde quotes from an old herbal: 'Also if thou be feeble boyle the leaves in cleane water and washe thyself and thou shalt wax shiny.' Among its many other virtues, rosemary stimulates the scalp and helps to relieve nervous headaches.

There should be a sunny nook in every garden for a rosemary bush. Starred with pale blue flowers nearly all the year round and with its narrow leaves green on one side and grey underneath, it is most attractive. The whole plant, especially the seeds, contains natural oils. This makes it valuable to use in the making of pot-pourri, hair rinses, toilet waters and scented rubbing lotions. Candied rosemary flowers, rosemary wine, rosemary honey and rosemary snow were once favoured confections. Today we know of it as a popular herb in Italian cooking, and the leaves used sparingly are excellent in certain food.

There are several types: a rare gilded-leaved plant; a double-flowering kind; another with white flowers; one with broad leaves; a rosemary with horizontal branches which is valuable for rockery work; and the well-known bushy, upright rosemary which is the type most frequently used for seasoning. With the attractive symmetry of its narrow leaves and its rather stiff growing habit, this types makes a decorative hedge of medium height.

Rosemary will grow from seed, but it is quicker and easier to propagate from semi-hardwood cuttings, taken with a heel if possible, at any time of the year – August and September being the best months. It will flourish in a well-drained sunny position, sheltered from prevailing winds. Do not prune heavily; if you are using and cutting it quite frequently once it is an established bush, this is all it needs.

Rosemary leaves with their fresh pungent flavour give a delicious fragrance to food, particularly lamb, veal, pork and beef. As the leaves are thin and spiky, it is essential to cut them

Rosemary

up finely. This is easily done by holding as many as you can gather in your fingers, and then cutting them with the kitchen scissors into a container. When putting a sprig in to boil with pickled pork, corned beef or salted mutton it is not necessary to do this as the leaves are merely used to impart flavour.

When dried, the leaves become crisp and brittle, and are easily crumbled or chopped. When added to a scone mixture it gives the scones a delicious flavour; it may often be used instead of thyme, and is excellent in pea soup, minestrone, spinach soup, and in casseroles and stews, or added to the water for boiling pickled pork. A recipe for Rosemary Tea is given on page 165.

CASSEROLE OF BEEF
(A Mediterranean recipe)

- 4 lb. beef
- ½ lb. bacon cut into fairly big pieces
- 1 cup of oil
- 2 cloves garlic
- 2 peeled tomatoes
- 1 dozen stoned black olives
- 1 dessertspoon rosemary
- 1 wine glass red wine
- salt and pepper

Cut the beef into thick rounds. Heat the oil in a fireproof dish on top of the stove, put in the meat and seal on both sides. Lower the heat and add the bacon, garlic and tomatoes. Simmer a little longer, and add the rosemary, olives, salt, pepper and wine. Put the lid on the dish and cook in a slow oven for 2 hours.

BEEF AND TOMATOES

In this hearty dish, also from the Mediterranean, the juices from the meat and vegetables mingle with the herbs and wine to form a savoury and aromatic sauce.

- 1½ lb. shin of beef, roughly cut up
- 3 rashers of bacon, cut in squares
- 1 glass white or red wine
- 4 tomatoes, peeled
- 2 cloves of garlic, sliced
- 2 onions, peeled and sliced
- 1 dessertspoon chopped rosemary
- 1 bay leaf
- 10 juniper berries, crushed
- salt and pepper

Rosemary

Put the meat into a casserole and cover it with the squares of bacon, then add the remaining ingredients. Bake with the lid on in a slow oven (gas ½–1, electric 250–300°F.) for 3 to 4 hours.

BUTTERED CABBAGE SPINES AND ROSEMARY

A new and delicious vegetable was introduced to us by my aunt and uncle: in fact, two vegetables are made from one. The pale-green 'spines' are cut from the leaves of a cabbage with a pair of sharp kitchen scissors, giving a mound of crisp stalks and another of soft leaves with no stalks. Wrap these leaves in foil and put in the refrigerator for another occasion (they may be shredded finely and steamed for a few minutes with a knob of butter). Put the cabbage spines or stalks into a saucepan with water and a little salt, bring to the boil, and simmer until they are tender (this may take from 20 to 30 minutes). Drain the stalks and pour over them a mixture of melted butter and 2 teaspoons of finely chopped or crumbled rosemary.

ROSEMARY SNOW

One of the prettiest conceits from sophisticated Tudor days was Rosemary Snow.

(in *A Garden of Herbs*, by E. S. Rohde, from *A Book of Fruits and Flowers*, 1653)

'Take a quart of thick Creame, and five or six whites of Eggs, a saucer full of Sugar finely beaten and as much Rosewater, beat them all together and always as it riseth take it out with a spoon, then take a loaf of Bread, cut away the crust, set it in a platter, and a great Rosemary bush in the middest of it, then lay your Snow with a Spoon upon the Rosemary, and so serve it.'

ROSEMARY SCONES

I have often served these scones to people who are interested in the unique flavour that herbs give to everyday food. As there could be nothing more everyday than scones, and as the recipe has been so popular, here it is.

Roses

    8 oz. self-raising flour
    a pinch each of salt and sugar
    1 tablespoon butter
    1 tablespoon finely chopped rosemary
    ⅓ pint milk

Sift the flour with the salt and sugar, rub in the butter, add the rosemary, then the milk. Mix to a soft dough, roll lightly, and cut into squares. Place the squares close together on a greased and floured baking sheet, and bake in a hot oven (gas 7, electric 425 °F.) for about 15 minutes.

Dried rosemary may be moistened before being chopped; or you can crumble it between your fingers.

ROSEMARY HAIR RINSE

Pick a bunch of rosemary, cover it well with water and simmer it for ½ hour or more. A delicate fragrance and a tonic effect is given to the hair when given a final rinse with this preparation.

Roses

While we are talking of herbs and their uses, we must not overlook roses. They were once of supreme importance in a garden: not only were they admired for their beauty, but they were considered so useful that instead of being allowed to fall or wither away, they were collected and used in many ways. There are countless old recipes involving roses: rose syrup and rose vinegar, oil of roses, rose water, rose-scented snuff, candied rose petals, rosehip syrup, rose honey, rose 'cakes', sweet sachets, pot-pourri and rose-petal jam and jelly.

Roses have been loved by the human race for centuries, and the most scented of all, the damask rose, was said to have been brought from Damascus by the Crusaders. We still love roses for their beauty and fragrance, and new varieties are grown every year, but whatever one's personal choice may be, they are essential in a garden.

The eglantine of Chaucer and Shakespeare is the sweet briar rose, and it is the name Chaucer gives to his Prioress in *The Canterbury Tales*:

Roses

There was also a nun, a Prioress
Whose smile was simple, quiet, even coy.
The only oath she swore was, 'By Saint Loy!'
And she was known as Sister Eglantine.

Constance Spry in her *Constance Spry Cookery Book* gives many recipes for using roses in cooking. She suggests that a spoonful or two of rose jam or jelly added to certain sweets and ices gives them a delicious perfume and flavour.

ROSE-PETAL JAM
(from *Herbs and Herb Gardening*, by Eleanour Sinclair Rohde)

'It is essential to use red, fragrant Roses. To fifty fully opened Roses allow two pints of water, preferably clean rainwater or distilled water, and 3 lb. of the best preserving sugar. Boil the sugar and water till it candies a little. Add the juice of a small Lemon and the Rose petals. Stir well and bring to the boil. Put in a pat of butter to clear the scum and then simmer for quite an hour. It is necessary to stir very frequently, every five minutes or so, or the colour will be brown instead of red. Pour into pots and cover when cold.'

I have made this recipe using ordinary tap water, and it really makes quite a large quantity.

ROSE VINEGAR

Fill a glass or crockery vessel with petals from scented roses and pour 1 pint of wine vinegar over them. Cover and allow to infuse for 2 weeks, preferably in the sun. Strain, and use in the same way as tarragon vinegar.

GREEN SALAD WITH ROSE PETALS

When ready to serve a lettuce salad, toss with a French dressing made with rose-petal vinegar, add 1 tablespoon of rose petals from the tiny roses (or the smallest petals from scented roses) and mix again. Excellent for a luncheon with cold poultry.

CANDIED ROSE PETALS

Make sure the rose petals are not bruised and are thoroughly dry. Coat each one carefully with beaten white of egg applied with a small clean paint brush. Dust with castor sugar. Turn them over and repeat the process. Dry in the sun, occasionally turning them. When they are quite dry store in airtight jars between layers of greaseproof paper.

I can remember only pink ones being used; they were delicious on trifles with sugared violets and silver cashews nestling on whipped cream. They may also be used for decorating cakes.

HONEY OF ROSES

(in *A Garden of Herbs*, by E. S. Rohde, and from an old recipe by T. Tryon in *A Treatise of Cleanness in Meates*, 1692)

'Cut the white heels from Red Roses, take half a pound of them and put them into a stone jar, and pour on them three pints of boiling water. Stir well and let them stand twelve hours. Then press off the liquor, and when it has settled add to it five pounds of honey. Boil it well, and when it is of the consistence of a thick syrup it is ready to put away.'

POT-POURRI

To about 40 roses allow the following spices and oils:

½ oz. *oil of geranium*	1 oz. *ground nutmeg*
½ oz. *oil of lavender*	1 oz. *coriander seed*
2 or 3 *cinnamon sticks*	4 oz. *orris root powder*
1 oz. *whole cloves*	about 4 oz. *common salt*

Gather the roses on a dry day after the dew has left them. Spread them out in a cool, airy place, turning them frequently. When the petals are paper-dry put them with the salt into a crockery or glass vessel with an airtight lid. To each handful of petals allow a smaller one of salt.

Cover and leave, stirring twice a day for 5 days. In the meantime, gather all the scented leaves and flowers that are suitable, about a handful of each according to what is available and personal taste. Scented geranium leaves, particularly the rose-scented, are excellent, as well as lavender flowers, rosemary flowers, carnations, bay leaves, lemon-scented verbena, balm, jasmine, eau-de-Cologne mint, orange blossoms, violets and wallflowers.

These should be drying on sieves or on sheets of paper. On the fifth day add these ingredients to the roses and salt.

Put some of the orris powder in a cup and add the oils, stirring well until the consistency is no longer moist but powdery. A chemist advised me to do this, as the powder quickly 'takes up' the valuable oil which is then added to the pot-pourri with the rest of the orris powder and spices, and is evenly distributed. Dried sliced angelica root and a little orange and lemon peel, with no pith adhering to the skin, may be added too.

Stir all the ingredients very well, cover and leave for 3 or 4 weeks. It may be stirred occasionally, in fact it is a pleasure to do so.

If the pot-pourri becomes too dry add more salt, and if too moist add more orris root powder.

As the spices retain their strength for years, dried flowers may be added from time to time. Rosemary and lavender flowers are especially good as they contain essential aromatic oils. When put into suitable bowls this makes a delightful gift.

ROSE WATER

Nicholas Culpeper, the seventeenth-century herbalist, says of rose water in *Culpeper's Complete Herbal*: 'Red rose water is well known, and of a similar use on all occasions, and better than the damask rose water, it is cooling, cordial, refreshing, quickening the weak and faint spirits, used either in meats or broths, to wash the temples, to smell at the nose, or to smell the sweet vapours out of a perfume pot, or cast into a hot fire-shovel.'

There are many recipes for making rose water, but most of them are tedious and difficult with their instructions for distilling. The following recipe is quite simple. Some people use it in finger bowls, or put a little of it in a basin of water for guests to wash their hands.

Take 2 handfuls of scented red rose petals and put them in

a jug or earthen pot. Pour over them 2 pints of water and ½ lb. sugar. Let them steep for 1 hour. Take the water and roses and pour from one vessel into another until the water is scented with the flowers. Strain and keep in a cool place.

Saffron

Saffron (*Crocus sativus*) comes from the orange-coloured stigmas of a mauve-flowering crocus, native to Asia and parts of Europe. It is a rare and expensive spice because only the hand-picked stigmas are used, and it requires over 200,000 of these to make one pound; fortunately only a small quantity is needed to colour and flavour food.

Saffron has been prized from the most ancient times for use in food, medicine, and dyes; in *The Bible as History* we are told that the colourful garments of the Children of Israel owed their brightness to nature: saffron for yellow, madder-root for red, and the murex snail supplied purple.

Culpeper describes saffron as being a herb of the sun, and says: 'It refreshes the spirits, and is good against fainting-fits and the palpitation of the heart.' But he cautions against an immoderate amount being taken. Sir Francis Bacon thought so highly of this herb that he said: 'What made the English people sprightly was the liberal use of saffron in their broths and sweet-meats' (Eleanour Sinclair Rohde, *A Garden of Herbs*). In medieval days saffron was also popular as a dye for the hair.

This crocus was once grown extensively at Saffron Walden; the arms of the town have three saffron flowers pictured within turreted walls. Saffron Hill, now a London thoroughfare, was once part of the gardens of Ely Place, where quantities of saffron were grown.

The warmly bitter aroma and the gold colour of saffron give certain dishes their traditional flavour and colour: the saffron cakes of Cornwall are well known; saffron is an important ingredient in the classic French fish soup Bouillabaisse and in the Spanish Arroz con Pollo (Rice with Chicken) and Paëlla; it also enhances some sauces, breads, cakes, fish, chicken, and rice dishes.

Today saffron comes from different parts of the world and is almost as precious as gold dust. When ground to a russet powder it is packaged carefully in envelopes; it is also available in whole orange and gold threads. When using the threads, crush the required number and infuse in the hot milk or other liquid which the recipe calls for. The powder may be infused in liquid or sifted with flour.

SAFFRON RISOTTO

A delicately flavoured golden dish to serve with fricasseed chicken, fish or a veal casserole. This method of cooking a risotto is recommended provided the cooking time is watched and the quantities given are measured accurately.

2 oz. butter
1 medium-sized onion, chopped
1 clove of garlic, chopped
1 small green capsicum, chopped
½ lb. rice
1 pint chicken broth (may be made with chicken cubes)
¼ teaspoon saffron

Infuse the saffron, whether ground or whole, in the hot chicken broth. Melt the butter in a fireproof pan or casserole, add the onion, garlic and capsicum, then the rice, turning until the grains are shining and coated. Add the saffron-flavoured chicken broth. Bring to the boil, put the lid on, and place in a moderate oven (gas 4, electric 350°F.) to bake for 30 minutes.

SUNNY SAFFRON DUMPLINGS

4 oz. self-raising flour
a pinch of salt
2 oz. butter
2 teaspoons dried parsley
¼ cup milk
a pinch of powdered saffron

These dumplings are for a meat or chicken casserole.

Sift the flour and salt into a bowl, rub in the butter, and add the parsley. Heat the milk and saffron together, add to the flour, and mix to a firm dough. Pat out on a floured surface, and roll lightly. Mark deep incisions in the form of squares with a knife, slide in one piece on to the cooked, bubbling casserole, replace the lid, and cook for 20 minutes. Serve immediately.

BOUILLABAISSE

It is said that only in France may one taste real bouillabaisse, for the original recipe calls for several different kinds of fish that are not available in other countries. Nevertheless, there are many versions of this popular fish soup, and this one has a delicious and unusual flavour and aroma, is quite inexpensive, and is quickly prepared by even the busiest cook.

4 lb. boned, filleted fish cut into pieces	2 cloves of garlic, cut very fine
¼ pint olive oil	1 teaspoon saffron
4 tomatoes, peeled and chopped	1 wine-glass white wine
	½ teaspoon thyme
3 onions, peeled and chopped	a bay leaf
	freshly ground pepper
	1 teaspoon salt

Trout is excellent if available.

Heat the oil in a large casserole, and fry in it the tomatoes, onions, garlic and saffron, together with salt and pepper. Add the sliced fish, wine, thyme and bay leaf, cover with water (about 2 quarts), bring to the boil, and simmer for 10 minutes. Serve hot. Accompany with slices of French bread.

SAFFRON BUNS

An old recipe from an authority on English folk cookery, Florence White, who includes it in her collection, *Good English Food*.

Take 3½ lb. flour, ½ lb. butter, ½ pint cream of milk; set the milk on the fire, put in the butter and a good deal of sugar, strain saffron to your taste into the milk, take three or four eggs, with one yolk and one ounce of compressed yeast, put the milk to it when almost cold, with salt, and coriander seeds; knead them all together, make them up into small cakes, or buns, set them to rise and bake them in a quick oven.

Sage

To prepare the saffron take half a drachm and cut very fine with scissors, pour over half a cup of boiling water and steep overnight.

SAFFRON GOOSEBERRY SHORTCAKE

8 oz. self-raising flour
¼ teaspoon powdered saffron
¼ teaspoon salt
3 oz. brown sugar
¼ lb. butter or margarine
2 eggs, beaten
¼ pint milk
1 lb. gooseberries, or a 1-lb. tin
1 dessertspoon arrowroot, blended with a little milk

This is a refreshing sweet in summer. It may be eaten for afternoon tea if you wish.

Sift the flour, saffron and salt into a bowl, add the brown sugar, rub in the butter and add the eggs and milk. Spoon into a greased, lightly floured 8-inch recessed tin and bake in a hot oven (gas 6–7, electric 400°F.) for 15 minutes. Cool and turn on to a cake rack. Open the tin of gooseberries, drain the liquid into a saucepan and simmer it until it is reduced a little. Thicken it with the blended arrowroot, stir in the gooseberries, cool, and pour on to the shortcake. Serve with thick cream.

If fresh gooseberries are used, stew the fruit in the usual way, thickening the syrup with arrowroot when cooked.

Sage

Aromatic sage (*Salvia officinalis*, one of the Labiatae) is a perennial plant native to Mediterranean countries, the Romans having brought it to the lands they conquered. Several kinds are known today, each differing in the colour, flavour and shape of the leaves. There is a sage with purple-tinged leaves, a pineapple-flavoured sage, a white-flowering and a pink-flowering sage. As the purple-flowering grey-leaved sage is used most frequently, it is the one described here. Sun-loving, it will thrive for many years in a well-drained, sheltered position, but will wither and die if the soil and situation are not to its liking. The healthiest sage plant I have seen was over five years old; it was about four feet high, and was growing in front of a sunny brick wall.

It is one of the old favourites that has not been lost to us, probably because for centuries it was highly esteemed for its health-giving properties. 'Why should a man die who has sage in his garden?' is an old proverb. The old herbalists had great respect for it, and country folk included it in their daily diet. It is interesting to read old recipes for sage wine, sage tea, sage cream, and even sage tobacco. It was sometimes used as a flavouring in the making of bread, also of cheese; and there is at least one cheese on the market today that is flavoured with sage. The traditional Mixed Herbs contain sage as well as thyme and marjoram, and it is an ingredient in the classic Sage and Onion Stuffing for roast duck.

Sage prefers a light soil and a sunny position. When it has finished blooming cut off the flower stalks, and it will soon grow into a compact bush between two and three feet high. Eventually it is wise to put in new plants, and this is easily done by breaking roots off from the old bush, or by sowing the seed when it is ripe.

According to the old writers, sage leaves are at their most beneficial in the spring, before the flower stalks begin to lengthen. It is also the best time for drying this herb. The leaves are very pungent and slightly acrid, but they have a very pleasant flavour when cooked.

Halved, buttered tomatoes piled with small mounds of scented sage, and baked until tender, go well with grilled pork chops and apple sauce.

A sage-cheese spread is simply made by beating 4 teaspoons of fresh or 3 teaspoons of dried sage and a few drops of lemon juice into 4 oz. cream cheese.

Rub a joint of meat with sage before roasting it. Try sage as a seasoning for meat rissoles, meat loaf, cheese dishes, eggs and fish.

Leek pie with yeast pastry is an old favourite. The following recipe, Leek Tart with Sage, is delicious and simple to make.

Sage

It has a very delicate flavour and is more palatable to those who find onions too strong. It goes very well with cold meat (lamb or mutton particularly) served with red currant jelly, or a sharp apple jelly. It is also excellent on its own with a French salad, and may be eaten either hot or cold. When preparing leeks for cooking, cut off the roots and leaves, leaving about one inch of the green, and wash very well.

LEEK TART WITH SAGE

1 dozen leeks
¼ pint cream or top of the milk
1 egg
1 tablespoon chopped parsley
1 tablespoon finely chopped sage leaves
2 or 3 rashers of bacon
salt and pepper
short pastry

Cut the leeks into thin circles, put them in a saucepan with a little water and simmer gently until soft. Drain, and add the chopped herbs, the beaten egg and the cream, mixing it all together. Adjust the seasoning.

Line a lightly floured pie-dish with thinly rolled short pastry. Prick it well, and spoon in the leek mixture. Cut the bacon into small squares (after removing the rind) and arrange on top of the tart. Bake in a medium to hot oven for about 20 minutes.

The short pastry I make is a recipe from my husband's family, and is known as Emily's Pastry. Hers was so light that it almost blew away, and yet it was rich and full of flavour.

EMILY'S PASTRY

4 oz. self-raising flour
2 oz. butter
½ cup cold water with a little lemon juice added
pinch of salt (and a pinch of sugar if the pastry is used for sweets)

Sift the dry ingredients. Rub the butter and flour together with the finger-tips. Add the water gradually and mix lightly with a knife. Roll lightly. Place in a fairly hot oven for 20 minutes. Do not brown too quickly. Always open and close the oven door very gently – *never bang*.

Sage

ISABELLE'S SAGE AND CHEESE OMELETTE

4 oz. grated Cheddar cheese
½ pint milk
2 eggs, separated
3 oz. soft breadcrumbs
1 dessertspoon grated onion
2 teaspoons chopped sage
salt and pepper

This is an excellent luncheon or supper dish.

Warm the milk, and add it to the beaten egg-yolks and other ingredients (except the egg-whites). Add salt and pepper. Allow the mixture to stand for 1 hour. Fold in the whipped egg-whites. Bake in a buttered dish in a fairly moderate oven (gas 4, electric 350°F.) for 30 minutes.

WELSH RAREBIT WITH SAGE

Cheese flavoured with sage has been favoured by country people for years. Welsh rarebit made with beer and flavoured with sage makes a particularly appetizing Sunday night meal.

½ lb. grated tasty cheese
1 dessertspoon finely chopped sage leaves
½ pint beer
salt, pepper, ½ teaspoon mustard

Warm the beer in a saucepan, and gradually add the cheese, then the sage, salt, pepper and mustard. Stir well until the cheese has melted. Serve hot with triangles of hot buttered toast.

SAGE AND ONION STUFFING
(from Mrs Beeton's *Poultry and Game*)

Take 4 large onions, 10 sage leaves, ¼ lb. breadcrumbs, 1½ oz. butter, salt and pepper to taste, and 1 egg.

Peel the onions, put them into boiling water, let them simmer for 5 minutes or rather longer, and, just before they are taken out, put in the sage leaves for a minute or two to take off their rawness. Chop both these very fine, add the bread, seasoning and butter, and work the whole together with the yolk of an egg, when the stuffing will be ready for use. It should be rather highly seasoned, and the sage leaves should be very finely chopped. Many cooks do not parboil the onions in the manner just stated, but merely use them raw, but the stuffing then is not nearly so mild, and, to many tastes, its

Sage

strong flavour would be very objectionable. When made for goose, a portion of the liver of the bird, simmered for a few minutes and very finely minced, is frequently added to this stuffing; and where economy is studied, the egg and butter may be omitted.

This should be sufficient for 1 goose, or a pair of ducks.

SAGE BREAD

This sage-flavoured bread is well worth the small amount of time and effort spent in preparing it. As it is a particularly quick method, it could become a winter standby to accompany roast meat, casseroles and thick stews, or for Sunday night supper with bowls of hot soup. It is delicious with Camembert and coffee.

- ½ oz. dry yeast
- 3 tablespoons warm water
- 1 lb. plain flour
- 1 teaspoon salt
- 2 dessertspoons dried sage
- 1 teaspoon allspice
- 1 teaspoon celery seed
- 1 dessertspoon sugar
- ½ pint warm milk
- 1 oz. butter
- 1 lightly beaten egg

Dissolve the yeast in the warm water. Sift the flour and salt into a bowl, and mix in the sage, allspice, celery seed and sugar. Form a well in the centre and pour into it the warm (not hot) milk in which the butter has been melted, then the egg and the dissolved yeast. Mix lightly, turn out on to a floured surface, and knead. Put into a greased bowl, cover with a small blanket, and leave in a warm place to rise for 1 hour. Turn out on to a floured surface once more. (In cold weather, first stand the warmed bowl on the table for a few minutes so that there is not too great a drop in temperature for the dough when it is turned out on to the board.) Knead and shape into a cottage loaf or two small loaves, place on a greased baking sheet, and allow to stand for 15 minutes. Bake in a hot oven (gas 7, electric 425 °F.) for about 30 minutes. If the top is browning too much, cover with a sheet of tinfoil and reduce the oven temperature a little.

SAGE HAIR TONIC

Here is an old 'receipt' from *Lotions and Potions,* a collection of

Salt

their ancestors' recipes compiled by members of the Women's Institute:

Take 1 tablespoonful each of tea and of dried sage. Put into a 2-lb. jam jar, cover with boiling water, and simmer for 2 hours. Cool and strain. Rub into the scalp four or five times a week. Gradually greyness will disappear, and hair becomes dark brown. Will keep for a week; add 1 tablespoonful of rum, gin or eau-de-Cologne for longer keeping.

TO WHITEN THE TEETH

Rub with sage leaves. This hint also came from *Lotions and Potions*.

SAGE TEA

If you have sage and lemon balm growing, here is a wholesome old beverage quoted in *A Garden of Herbs* by Eleanour Sinclair Rohde from *The New Art of Cookery*, by Richard Briggs (many years Cook at the Globe Tavern, Fleet Street, The White Hart Tavern, Holborn, and at the Temple Coffee House, 1788): 'Take a little sage, a little Balm, put it into a pan, slice a Lemon, peel and all, a few knobs of sugar, one glass of white wine; pour on these two or three quarts of boiling water; cover it, and drink when thirsty. When you think it strong enough of the herbs take them out otherwise it will make it bitter.'

Salt

Salt is included here because it is essential in all types of cooking. Its value as an antiseptic and its use in medicine are well known.

Salt, or sodium chloride, occurs naturally in sea water; mineral deposits of rock salt are the crystalline evidence of vast salt lakes and seas long since vanished from the earth's surface. Smaller quantities are found near hot springs and mineral waters, the salt from the solution being precipitated and occurring in layers.

Savory

Refined free-running table salt (which has magnesium carbonate added to prevent it from caking) is seen on every grocer's shelf, as well as a coarser quality known as common salt. Some table salt has a proportion of iodine added to it as a preventive against goitre. Salt crystals (sea salt) for grinding over food should be put into a wooden salt mill as a companion to the pepper mill.

There are many seasoned salts which have gone through a process to capture the flavour required; some popular flavours at present are celery salt, garlic salt, mushroom salt, parsley salt, salt seasoned with spices and herbs, and health salt containing dehydrated vegetables and herbs.

A seasoned salt for the kitchen, barbecues, or the table is very useful: an interesting blend is easily made by a selection from the spice shelf. A pestle and mortar for grinding and pounding the ingredients together is needed, and whether it is made from marble or smooth wood it is a practical and handsome kitchen implement.

SEASONED SALT

Grind together in a mortar 1 teaspoon celery seed and 1 teaspoon dried rosemary. Add 1 teaspoon each of ground mace and paprika, $\frac{1}{2}$ teaspoon sugar, and 1 tablespoon table salt. Put in a small airtight bottle and use as required.

Savory

Summer savory (*Satureia hortensis*) and winter savory (*S. montana*) are the two popular varieties of this genus, from the Labiatae, for use in cooking. The Romans are believed to have introduced it to England, and it was so well liked that it was one of the herbs taken by the early settlers to America.

Seed of the summer savory, which is an annual, is sown in the spring, the plant growing to about one and a half feet high. Winter savory, a perennial, may be grown from seed also, but it is usually more satisfactory to divide the roots in the spring,

Savory

when it will grow rapidly into a bushy shrub a little over a foot high. Grow both varieties of savory in light soil in the sun. Winter savory is also a well-contented habitué of the window box. Do not plant it, however, with parsley or chives as it may take over the whole container.

The flavour is essentially the same in both varieties – peppery and aromatic, with the elusive scent of rosemary and the pungency of sage. The sturdy evergreen bushes of winter savory make an attractive low hedge for a herb garden, and it was put to great use in Tudor days for this purpose and for knot gardens and dwarf shrub mazes. Eleanour Sinclair Rohde says in *Herbs and Herb Gardening*: 'Hyll, in his *Proffitable Arte of Gardening* (1568), gives a plan for a dwarf shrub maze "and it may eyther be set with Isope and Tyme or with winter Savory and Tyme. For these do well endure all the winter through grene."'

At first glance the savories resemble thyme; however, on closer inspection, you will see that the leaves are longer and quite narrow. Like thyme the leaves are pungent, but with a hot peppery flavour. It is said that rubbing a leaf on a bee sting will relieve the pain.

Both summer savory and winter savory have been used for many years on the Continent in meat and fish dishes (it is supposed to be especially good with trout), in stuffings, and boiled with beans as mint is with peas. A Tudor custom was to mix dried savory with breadcrumbs giving a 'quicker relish' to crumbed fish or meat. With chopped chives and parsley it makes an excellent stuffing for duck. It is also a pleasant accompaniment for lamb, pork and veal, and gives a delightfully different flavour to tomato sauce.

Savory retains its flavour well when dried.

FRIED TRIPE AND WINTER SAVORY

1½ *lb. tripe*
1 *chopped white onion*
¼ *pint oil*
2 *thinly sliced cloves of garlic*
⅛ *pint stock*
1 *tablespoon fresh or*
1 *dessertspoon dried savory*
1 *tin or ½ lb. fresh mushrooms*
flour

Simmer the tripe for about an hour. Drain in a colander, allowing the cold tap to run over it. Fry the onion and garlic in the oil until soft. Cut the tripe into cubes, roll in flour and add to the onion and garlic. Fry until golden, adding more oil if necessary. Put in a fireproof dish, add the mushrooms, savory and ½ pint of stock. Cover and simmer in a slow oven for 1 hour. Even people who don't care for tripe usually like it this way.

BAKED FISH WITH CIDER

2 lb. fish fillets	3 finely sliced shallots
1 tablespoon finely chopped savory	1 breakfast cup cider
	soft breadcrumbs
2 peeled and cored apples cut into wedges	butter
	flour, salt and pepper

Roll the fillets in flour and put them in a buttered fireproof dish with the apple, savory and shallots. Season with salt and freshly ground pepper. Pour the cider in slowly and carefully. Top with breadcrumbs which have been lightly fried in butter. Bake in a moderate oven for about 20 minutes. The fragrance of apple and cider united with spicy savory combines well with fish.

SAVORY STUFFED LEG OF LAMB

1 small leg of lamb, boned	6 juniper berries, crushed
3 oz. soft breadcrumbs	a few pieces of butter
3 teaspoons fresh or 2 teaspoons dried savory	1 good glass red or white wine
1 dessertspoon chopped white onion	¼ lb. butter or margarine, melted
1 clove of garlic, finely chopped	salt and pepper

Mix together the breadcrumbs, savory, onion, garlic, crushed juniper berries and the pieces of butter, adding salt and pepper to taste. Stuff the leg, fasten it with skewers, and put it into a baking dish with the wine and the melted butter. Bake in a moderate oven (gas 4, electric 350–75°F.) for 1 to 1½ hours, basting frequently. Add a little more wine if necessary. To serve, lift the leg on to a hot dish and pour the pan juices over it. Surround with well-drained boiled potatoes coated with butter and chopped parsley.

SAVORY STUFFING FOR FISH

3 oz. soft breadcrumbs	2 oz. butter
grated rind and juice of 1 lemon	1 tablespoon finely chopped onion
1 dessertspoon finely chopped savory	1 egg
	salt and pepper

Soften the butter in a frying pan and gently fry the onion without browning. Add to the other ingredients in a bowl, binding the mixture with the egg. A dozen oysters or 1 cup shelled prawns may be added with advantage to the stuffing.

SAVORY TOMATO SAUCE

This is an excellent sauce with grills.

Peel and chop 1 lb. ripe tomatoes and simmer them in a saucepan with 1 finely chopped onion, 2 teaspoons dried savory or 3 of fresh and 1 cup water, adding salt and pepper to taste. When cooked, rub through a sieve. Melt 2 oz. butter, blend in 1 heaped tablespoon plain flour, and gradually add the sauce. Stir until thickened. Bottle.

SAVORY AND GRAPE-JUICE JELLY

A mellow and fragrant jelly to eat with turkey, ham and other meat dishes, equally delicious on buttered hot rolls and scones. The glowing colour reminds me of how the jelly described by Flora Thompson in *Lark Rise to Candleford* must have looked when ready to eat – jelly that was strained and sweetened and laced with port, sufficient to colour it a deep ruby, and cleared with eggshells, and strained again, then poured into a flannel jellybag and hung from a hook all night to let its contents ooze through, then poured into a mould and allowed yet one more night in which to set.

This recipe is delicious, and it is very easy to make.

1 bottle dark grape juice	4 oz. powdered pectin
2 dessertspoons dried savory	3 cups sugar
	juice of a lemon

Heat the grape juice and savory together, then add the pectin and bring to the boil. Add the sugar and lemon juice and boil for 2 minutes, stirring all the time. Remove from the stove, skim, and seal into small jars immediately.

Sesame Seed

Sesame (*Sesamum indicum*) is an annual herb that is grown as an important food crop in many parts of the world today. It grows three to four feet high and has white flowers that are followed by oil-bearing seeds high in protein and mineral content. The mature pods pop at the merest touch, scattering the small white seeds, and this makes harvesting with machinery difficult, though strains that do not have this tendency are now being grown.

Sesame is one of the earliest and most valuable herbs known to man. The name itself is associated with well-known fables, bringing to mind Ali Baba's magic words 'Open, Sesame!' and the revealing of that glowing, jewel-filled cave.

Dorothy Bovée Jones says in *The Herbarist*: 'There is some disagreement among authorities as to the exact center of origin for this ancient herb. It may have been Afghanistan, or Africa, or the Sunda Islands in the East Indies. It does not exist in a wild state today. It is mentioned in Sanskrit literature and in Egyptian scripts as well as in old Hebrew writings. Marco Polo wrote that he had had sesame oil in travelling through Persia, and thought it had a better flavour than any oil he had ever tasted.' Cleopatra, wise in the art of cosmetics, is supposed to have used sesame oil as a skin beautifier.

A product of sesame seed is an edible opaque cream known as tahina, which has the consistency of honey and in taste resembles peanut butter. It is extremely popular in Arabic, Egyptian, Lebanese and Greek food, and may be found in some Continental provision stores. Tahina mixed with cooked brown beans makes a Lebanese dish. Another favourite dish is made with cooked aubergine and tahina mashed to a paste:

it is eaten cold as an hors-d'œuvre with pieces of bread. Tahina is sometimes thinned with a little lemon juice to make a nutty sauce for fish and shellfish; it is also palatable and nourishing when spread straight from the container on to bread and butter.

Tahina is an ingredient in the confection named Halva, said to be Egyptian in origin and particularly popular with Greek, Syrian and Jewish people – and with anyone else once they have tasted it. When chilled and cut into small blocks it makes an agreeable accompaniment to black coffee. Delicatessens usually keep it.

Sesame meal, which is ground sesame seed, is obtained from health-food shops; because it is so high in protein, vegetarians use quantities of it in their daily diet. The meal is used in various ways: it is sprinkled on salads and vegetables, and together with eggs and desiccated coconut it makes sustaining and pleasant-tasting little cakes.

Sesame seed and honey bars are delectable candies to be found in delicatessens and cake shops. In fact, the flavour of sesame has a powerful attraction, and anything made with the seed, or any product from it, is delicious.

There are many quick and simple ways in which sesame seed may be introduced into everyday food:

Gently fry a tablespoon of sesame seed in butter until light brown, and either toss through a green salad or add to whipped potato, cream cheese or mashed savoury avocado.

Toast the seed lightly and sprinkle it on cooked chicken and fish, cream soups and fruit salads.

Sprinkle sesame seed on uncooked foods like scones, biscuits, cookies, rolls or casseroles; the seed will brown during cooking.

Use sesame seed wherever you would use nuts in cooking, for a change.

SESAME-SEED SALAD

1 head of lettuce	2 tablespoons sesame seed
½ cup stoned black olives	butter
2 tomatoes, quartered	French dressing (page 158)

Tarragon

Wash and dry the lettuce, tear the leaves and put them into a salad bowl. Add the olives and tomatoes. Gently fry the sesame seed in butter until it is golden, add to the salad, and toss well with French dressing.

AUBERGINE AND TAHINA APPETIZER

This is delicious when served with thin slices of rye bread.

Peel and cut up an aubergine. Fry gently in butter until soft – about 10 minutes. Turn into a bowl and mash to a pulp, or put into a blender. Add 1 teaspoon salt, 1 tablespoon lemon juice, 2 pulverized cloves of garlic, $\frac{1}{4}$ cup tahina, and 1 dessertspoon chopped mint. Blend all together.

Put the mixture into a dish and chill in the refrigerator, where it will set firm.

SESAME AND OATMEAL COOKIES

4 oz. rolled oats	1 teaspoon salt
$\frac{1}{4}$ cup sesame seed	$\frac{3}{4}$ cup desiccated coconut
4 oz. demerara sugar	$\frac{1}{4}$ lb. butter, melted

These are popular with children. To make, mix all the dry ingredients together, add the melted butter and stir it into the mixture. Press out on to a greased and floured tray. Bake in a moderate oven (gas 5–6, electric 375–400°F.) for 30 minutes. Cut into fingers when cold.

Tarragon

This perennial herb (*Artemisia dracunculus* from the Compositae) is native to Europe and parts of Asia. There are two accepted culinary types, known as French tarragon and Russian tarragon. While the latter sets seed and is easy to cultivate, it is generally thought that the flavour is not as good as that of French tarragon, which is prized by cooks. The particular aroma of French tarragon suits certain food to perfection; the plant, however, is usually grown only from cuttings or root division, and hardly ever sets seed. Soil and climatic conditions change the taste of the leaves considerably, even when cuttings are taken from a parent plant with an excellent flavour. Grow the plant in light, rather poor soil in a warm position, allowing it to absorb as much sunlight as possible.

Tarragon belongs to the same family as those famous and interesting herbs wormwood, southernwood, cudweed and mugwort; these are all artemisias, and have long been valued for their medicinal properties.

Wormwood is an ingredient in the making of the French liqueur absinthe, and it is also used in certain medicines.

Cudweed was called Live-for-ever and Herbe Impious, the reason for the last name being given in Gerard's Herbal (1597): '... those floures which appeare first ... are overtopt by other floures, which come on younger branches, and grow higher as children seeking to overgrow or overtop their parents (as many wicked children do), for which cause it hath been called "Herbe Impious".' It is said to be 'Dian's bud' which Oberon used to waken Titania in *A Midsummer Night's Dream*.

Mugwort has a fascinating history in early folklore and was regarded as having mystic qualities.

Nearly every English cottage garden had a bush of southernwood, also known as Lad's Love or Old Man. It is a three-foot-high ornamental shrub with the most delicate grey-green foliage. Bitter-sweet describes the scent and flavour of this herb. It is very aromatic with a slight touch of ether about it. Perhaps this is why it was once a remedy for insomnia! Its peculiar antiseptic smell repels moths, and it has medicinal virtues as well. Of this unusual and appealing plant Edward Thomas writes in his poem 'Old Man':

> *Old Man, or Lad's-love – in the name there's nothing*
> *To one that knows not Lad's-love, or Old Man,*
> *The hoar-green feathery herb, almost a tree,*
> *Growing with rosemary and lavender.*
> *Even to one that knows it well, the names*
> *Half decorate, half perplex, the thing it is:*
> *At least, what that is clings not to the names*
> *In spite of time. And yet I like the names.*

Tarragon is the most palatable of the artemisias. It is tartly

Tarragon

aromatic, and its uses in the kitchen are many. It is usual to add a little chopped tarragon to such sauces as Hollandaise, Béarnaise and Tartare. Tarragon gives chicken stuffing a delightfully different flavour. It is excellent in fish and shellfish dishes, in veal and rabbit dishes, with chicken livers, and in chicken or fish soups. It may be added to sour cream sauces, mayonnaise and French dressing. When using the dried herb, which is more aromatic than the fresh, chop it finely and begin with 1 teaspoon unless otherwise stated in the recipe: a little more can then be added according to taste.

CHICKEN LIVERS IN WINE

- 1½ lb. chicken livers
- ¼ lb. butter
- 2 cloves of garlic, finely chopped
- 1 teaspoon dried or 2 teaspoons fresh marjoram
- 2 teaspoons chopped tarragon
- 1 tablespoon plain flour
- ½ pint red or white wine
- salt and pepper

Wash the chicken livers, cut in half and simmer gently in the butter with the garlic until cooked. Add the tarragon, marjoram and flour, season with salt and pepper, and turn the livers until the flour browns. Gradually add the wine, stirring until the gravy is smooth and thickened. Serve with boiled rice.

CHICKEN SUPRÊME WITH PEACHES

- 1 fowl
- 2 tablespoons butter
- 1½ tablespoons flour
- 1 egg
- ¼ pint thick cream
- 4 ripe peaches
- 2 tablespoons finely chopped tarragon
- salt and pepper

Put the fowl on a wire sieve in a large saucepan and steam it gently until it is tender. Lift out, cut into pieces and arrange on a large plate. Keep it warm. Melt the butter, add the flour, stirring until it is well blended. Gradually add ¾ pint of the stock in which the chicken was cooked and stir until it thickens. Adjust the seasoning. Beat the egg and cream together and pour into the sauce. Stir for ½ minute, remove from the stove,

Tarragon

and mask the chicken with it. Peel and cut the peaches into halves, poach gently, drain and arrange around the chicken. Sprinkle with tarragon and serve very hot. If fresh peaches are not available, the best tinned peaches will do.

CRAB AND AVOCADO MOULD

- 2 cups crabmeat
- 2 avocadoes peeled and diced
- 1 cup diced celery
- 1 tin tomato soup
- 1½ tablespoons gelatine
- 1 tablespoon chopped tarragon
- salt and pepper

Mix the crabmeat, avocado, tarragon and celery together; adjust the seasoning. Soak the gelatine in ½ cup of heated tomato soup for 5 minutes, and then stir it slowly into the remainder of the soup. Pour this over the crabmeat mixture and set it in a mould. When firm, turn it out on a bed of watercress or finely shredded lettuce surrounded by slices of lemon.

SAUCE TARTARE

- 1 egg-yolk
- ¼ pint olive oil
- 1 tablespoon tarragon vinegar
- 1 teaspoon chopped capers (optional)
- 1 dessertspoon chopped olives
- 1 dessertspoon chopped tarragon
- a little mustard
- salt and pepper

Put the egg-yolk into a basin with the mustard, salt and pepper. Drop the oil on to this gradually, stirring well all the time until the mixture is smooth and thick. Beat in the vinegar carefully and add the olives, tarragon and capers. Serve with fish.

HOLLANDAISE SAUCE

Hollandaise and Béarnaise sauce are similar in composition. Other well-known sauces, such as Mousseline and Choron, are based on these two, the ingredients that make the variation being added at the end.

There are several methods of making Hollandaise, but I have found the following recipe the most satisfactory. It is important to have all ingredients to hand. If you haven't a double saucepan, a bowl stood in gently boiling water will do instead.

Tarragon

2 egg-yolks
1 tablespoon cream
1 dessertspoon lemon juice
1 tablespoon water

¼ lb. butter
1 teaspoon chopped tarragon
salt and pepper

Into a small bowl within easy reach of the stove put the yolks, cream, lemon juice and water, with salt and pepper to taste. When water is boiling gently in the bottom half of a double saucepan, melt the butter in the top half, then with a wire whisk beat in the contents of the small bowl. Continue beating until the mixture thickens, then remove immediately from the heat, beating a little longer to prevent curdling (if this happens, quickly beat in a few drops of cold water and another egg-yolk). Add the tarragon.

Hollandaise sauce should be served lukewarm. It may be poured into the cavity of ripe, stoned avocado pears for an entrée. It is delicious with asparagus, young beans, grilled fish and other finely textured food.

CHICKEN MIMOSA

Steam a chicken until the flesh is tender. Keep the chicken stock for making the sauce. Remove the flesh from the bones while the bird is still hot, and cut into thin slices. Make a stuffing by mixing together 2 cups soft breadcrumbs, 3 teaspoons seasoning herbs, 1 dessertspoon chopped tarragon, 1 dessertspoon chopped shallots and a little grated lemon rind, adding salt and pepper to taste. Spread this mixture in the bottom of a buttered fireproof dish and lay the chicken slices on it.

Make Sauce Suprême by melting in a saucepan ¼ lb. butter, blending in ½ cup plain flour, and gradually adding 1½ pints chicken stock. Stir until thickened. Lightly beat together 5 eggs, ¼ pint cream and a sprinkling of salt and pepper. Pour a little of the thickened chicken liquid from the saucepan on to these eggs, then add this mixture to the saucepan. Allow to cook for a few minutes (do not boil), stirring all the time. Now pour the sauce over the chicken pieces in the fireproof dish. Bake in a slow oven (gas 1, electric 300°F.) for about

Thyme

45 minutes, or until the sauce has set. Sprinkle the top with the sieved yolks of 2 hard-boiled eggs.

This dish may be made in advance and gently heated through in the oven before being served hot with French-style peas (page 105) and Saffron Risotto (page 132). The fruity flavour of white burgundy is an ideal companion for this rich and savoury dish.

TARRAGON VINEGAR

Tarragon vinegar is quickly made. Pack a glass jar with tarragon leaves, pour wine vinegar over, cover and infuse for two weeks. Strain and pour into bottles. A fresh branch of tarragon put into the bottle not only adds strength to the vinegar, but looks effective.

If you have no fresh tarragon growing, steep 1 heaped tablespoon of dried tarragon leaves in 1 pint of wine vinegar. Leave for at least 2 weeks before using. The tarragon need not be strained off.

Thyme

This well-loved plant (*Thymus vulgaris*, from the Labiatae) is a perennial originating from the Mediterranean countries. There are numerous species, of different shapes and sizes, which gardeners delight in collecting, not only for the herb garden, but also for rockeries and to cover inhospitable ground. Those most popular for the kitchen are the grey, shrubby garden thyme, and the green-leaved, refreshing lemon-scented thyme. Garden thyme has been used in many savoury and nourishing dishes for hundreds of years. With other good cooking herbs, it was hung in fragrant bunches to dry in the stillroom or kitchen, and when needed, the dry leaves would be rubbed off and used on their own, or mixed with sage and marjoram.

Thyme is truly the enchanted herb. E. S. Rohde declares

Thyme

that 'wild thyme has always been a favourite with fairies' and she goes on to give an old recipe 'to enable one to see the Fairies'. It is directed that the 'vial glasse in which the liquid is made must first be washed with rose-water and marygolde water', and the flowers gathered towards the east from the side of a fairy throne.

Bees have always loved this herb, and honey made from it is the most delicious and fragrant of all. Thyme was always planted near the bee-hives and the hives were also rubbed with it.

Thyme is very easy to grow; propagate by root division, or strike cuttings in sand in late winter; grow the plants in light, well-drained soil in a sunny position and you will be rewarded by a spreading, thickly foliaged little plant in a very short time.

In spring and summer the scented flowers of the different varieties shade from reddish purple through soft lilac and pink to white. Although each variety has its own individuality of perfume, flavour and form, they are all aromatic. The volatile oil from this herb, thymol, is extracted and used in industry. In Roman times this herb was a remedy for melancholy, and today a tea made from the leaves is regarded as being invigorating and refreshing. Nicholas Culpeper, the early-seventeenth-century herbalist, says: 'A strong infusion, drank as tea, is pleasant, and a very effectual remedy for head-ache, giddiness, and other disorders of that kind; and a certain remedy for that troublesome complaint, the night-mare.'

The number of different thymes are too numerous to list, the following varieties being the most easily obtainable at present.

Garden thyme (*Thymus vulgaris*) is the species most often used in flavouring. It is a particularly savoury herb, growing into a shrubby plant about one foot high, with pale, creamy-pink flowers in spring. It dries very successfully; harvest the branches just before the plant flowers and hang up in a shady place for two or three weeks. Rub the dry leaves off the brittle stalks and store in airtight glass jars. The pungency of your own dried thyme surpasses that of any bought kind.

Thyme

Lemon thyme (*T. citriodorus*) is aptly named, having a delicious lemon scent overlaying the typical thymy flavour. The leaves are softer and rounder than garden thyme, and are therefore more satisfactory to use in cooking when picking sprays straight from the garden; it is also valuable when dried. The plant grows to a height of twelve inches and has fragrant pink flowers in spring and all through the summer, the colour of a moss-rose.

Variegated thyme (*T. citriodorus variegatus*) has green leaves with white or gold variegation and a definite lemon scent also. It may be used both as an ornamental plant and in cooking; it grows to twelve inches high and has pink flowers.

Caraway thyme (*T. herba-barona*) has a creeping habit and pink flowers. It has an unmistakable scent, redolent of caraway, and may be used in the kitchen to give a subtle flavour to certain food. The leaves stripped from the stalk give a fresh and piquant flavour to sandwiches cut very thinly and spread first with smooth scrambled egg.

T. nitidus is a fascinating little plant particularly suitable for rocky niches and those small spaces that should be left when flagging a terrace. It grows up into a little green hillock, looking rather like a spreading miniature bonsai tree, and in summer it is powdered with pale, mauve-tinted flowers.

T. pauciflorus is a strong-growing carpeting thyme with green foliage and soft pink flowers; it is excellent for rockeries and borders.

T. serpyllum is reputed to be Shakespeare's 'wild thyme', and because of its magic associations is a magic herb; Culpeper calls it 'Mother of thyme'. It has a vigorous creeping habit, is very fragrant and covered with bright pink flowers in summer. It looks most attractive growing around the sundial in a herb garden. This is the variety which is recommended for use in a thyme lawn (see page 17), and for making a fragrant garden seat: put earth where you desire your scented seat to be, and then plant the thyme in the early spring to form a dense mat, which it does very quickly.

T. serpyllum coccineous is very similar to the above but with a greater profusion of flowers.

Thyme

T. serpyllum lanuginosus has tiny woolly leaves, delicately scented. It forms a thick, grey carpet which is most effective for a rockery. It grows nicely on top of a herb-garden wall where it will fall in thin silver strands over the golden stones.

T. serpyllum albus is a carpeting thyme with green foliage and drifts of white flowers in the spring.

Westmorland thyme grows to two feet with soft mauve flowers. Edna Walling describes it as 'One of the most perfect of all edging plants ... Westmorland thyme, a variety of *T. serpyllum* which is mid-way between *T. vulgaris*, the common culinary thyme (an excellent carpeting and edging plant by the way) and the ground clinging *T. serpyllum* known variously as Shepherd's thyme and Mother of thyme.'

Thyme is used to flavour meat dishes, soups, bread stuffings, forcemeat, and some vegetables such as aubergines, mushrooms, onions, beetroot and courgettes. The green leaves may be stripped from the stalks and used in place of dried thyme for a change, but the aroma of this herb is more penetrating when dried.

RABBIT COOKED IN MILK

1 *rabbit*	1 *pint milk*
2 *tablespoons flour*	*salt and pepper*
4 *oz. butter or*	1 *tablespoon dried thyme or*
1 *small cup of oil*	2 *tablespoons fresh chopped*
2 *finely chopped onions*	*thyme*

Cut the rabbit into pieces and roll in the flour. Heat the butter or oil and gently fry the floured rabbit on both sides. Put the rabbit, onions and thyme in layers in a fireproof dish, seasoning as you go with salt and pepper. Pour in 1 pint of milk, cover the dish and cook in a moderately slow oven for 2 hours.

We have been enjoying this recipe ever since the war years when meat was rationed and rabbit was very popular and cooked in many different ways.

SAVOURY MEAT LOAF

½ *lb. minced bacon*	¼ *pint milk*
1 *lb. minced steak*	*salt and pepper*

Thyme

1½ oz. white breadcrumbs
1 chopped onion
1 egg
2 teaspoons dried thyme or
1 tablespoon fresh chopped thyme

Put the minced steak and bacon into a bowl and add the breadcrumbs, onion, thyme, salt and pepper. Work it well together with a fork, add the milk and the egg, blending the whole mixture. Turn it into a loaf tin and bake in a moderate oven for 1 hour.

SAVOURY MEAT BALLS IN SAUCE

Sauce: Simmer together for 15 minutes 1½ pints water, 1 onion, 1 bay leaf, a few black peppercorns, a pinch of salt and 2 beef cubes. Remove the onion and bay leaf. The mixture is now ready for the meat balls (the sauce is thickened at a later stage).

Meat Balls: Mix together 1½ lb. sausage meat or minced steak, 1 egg (beaten), 1 onion (finely chopped), 2 teaspoons dried thyme and a little salt and pepper. With well-floured hands form the mixture into balls and drop them into the sauce. Simmer for 30 minutes. Remove the meat balls and keep them hot in a dish.

Thicken the sauce with 1 dessertspoon cornflour blended with a little milk. Add chopped parsley, and pour this sauce over the meat balls. Serve hot.

CHICKEN MOULD

When the weather is hot and days are long and sunny, this smooth chicken mould is fragrant and cooling.

Simmer a chicken. Reserve the stock (about 3 cups). For the béchamel sauce, take 3 cups of chicken stock, melt 3 oz. butter in a saucepan, add 3 tablespoons plain flour, and blend; gradually pour in the stock with 1 cup milk added, stirring continuously. Put the béchamel on one side. Soften 2 envelopes gelatine in ½ cup hot water and stir until dissolved, then add to the béchamel sauce, mixing thoroughly. Add at once the following ingredients: 3 cups cooked chopped chicken, 2 tablespoons finely chopped shallot, 2 tablespoons chopped red capsicum, a little salt and pepper, ½ cup whipped cream, 1 tablespoon lemon juice, 1 teaspoon dried thyme and ¼ teaspoon nutmeg. Chill until beginning to thicken, turn into a rinsed-out mould, and set in the refrigerator. Unmould on to a flat dish and surround with sprigs of thyme and cress.

BUTTERED BABY MARROWS

Slice some fresh baby marrows (courgettes or zucchini) thinly. Place in a saucepan with 1 oz. butter, some salt and pepper and 1 teaspoon dried thyme. Cover, and cook gently till soft. The vegetable must not be allowed to burn in the beginning; if necessary, add a little more butter. The flavour is so delicate that this may be served as an entrée or eaten between courses.

THYME STUFFING FOR POULTRY

3 oz. white breadcrumbs
2 oz. butter
1 tablespoon finely chopped onion
grated rind and juice of 1 lemon
salt and freshly ground pepper
1 tablespoon thyme
1 dessertspoon chopped parsley
1 dessertspoon chopped marjoram
1 egg

Soften the onion in a frying pan in the butter without browning. Put all the ingredients in a bowl, binding them together with the egg.

TURKEY STUFFING

This recipe for a stuffing for a 15-lb. roast turkey was given to me by Mr and Mrs R. E. Allen, neighbours whose family have lived in the same district for 120 years. Their old stone house has high, cool ceilings, wide verandas and an old fireplace where a large black saucepan used to hang by a chain and hook.

Grate into a large bowl 8 cups soft breadcrumbs. Rub in ¼ lb. butter, add 1 onion (grated), 3 sticks celery (grated), 1 lb. raw pork (finely minced), the grated rind and juice of a lemon, 1 apple (grated), one 1-lb. tin crushed pineapple (drained), 2 eggs, ½ cup chopped parsley, 1 tablespoon dried thyme and a little salt and pepper. Mix all ingredients together (the consistency should be crumbly). Before stuffing the bird, rub the cavity with garlic.

Turmeric

The pineapple juice may be mixed with the fat to baste the turkey.

Turmeric

Turmeric (*Curcuma longa*) is a perennial plant of the ginger family, native to India and other parts of Asia. The dried, aromatic root is ground to a brilliant yellow powder which gives a commercial curry blend its typical colour and much of its flavour; it is used in the East as a dye for cottons and silks as well as for flavouring food.

The vivid hue and pungent scent of this spice seem essentially Eastern in character: 'What is the scent of a Bazaar? Who can say? ... Taking it as a whole, however, I fancy the smell of turmeric brings back more than anything else the wonderful kaleidoscope of colours in an Indian bazaar' (*India*, by Mortimer Menpes).

The mellow fragrance and bright colour of turmeric has made it popular as an ingredient in pickles and chutneys, and in mustard-powder blends. A small amount may be used for colouring cakes, and it is excellent in rice dishes; turmeric is often added to fish kedgeree, devilled eggs, French dressings and fish stews; a pinch stirred into a smooth white sauce gives colour and an elusive, rather peppery, taste.

KEDGEREE

This is a good luncheon or breakfast dish, which may be prepared the night before it is needed.

- 1 cup cooked rice
- 1 lb. any one of the following: smoked and flaked cooked cod or haddock, tinned salmon or tuna, prawns or lobster
- ¼ lb. butter or margarine
- 1 onion, peeled and chopped
- 1 capsicum, chopped
- 2 cloves of garlic, chopped
- 2 teaspoons turmeric
- juice of a lemon
- ½ teaspoon ground ginger
- salt and pepper
- 2 hard-boiled eggs, shelled
- 1 teaspoon dried parsley

Vanilla Pod

Melt the butter and soften the onion, capsicum and garlic in it. Add the turmeric, lemon juice, ginger and a little salt and pepper. Lightly stir in the fish and rice, and when thoroughly mixed together turn into a dish and heat in the oven before serving. Garnish with the eggs cut into circles, and with parsley.

TROPICAL POTATO SALAD

3 cups diced cooked potatoes
1 cup banana circles
1 cup finely chopped shallots (include the green part)
a little lemon juice
2 teaspoons turmeric
1 cup mayonnaise
2 hard-boiled eggs, sliced
salt and pepper

This salad has a pleasant and subtle combination of flavours.

Sprinkle lemon juice over the banana circles to prevent discoloration. While the potatoes are still warm, season them with salt and pepper and add the banana and shallot. Blend the turmeric with the mayonnaise and mix gently through the salad. Add the egg slices last. Chill before serving.

FRENCH DRESSING

Take 1 tablespoon of lemon juice or wine vinegar and blend in 2 tablespoons of olive or vegetable oil, some freshly ground pepper, a little salt, a pinch of sugar and a few grains of mustard powder. Prepare well in advance and keep in a small screw-top jar or covered jug until the last moment, before the salad is tossed, when the mixture should be thoroughly stirred or vigorously shaken.

This dressing is also used as a marinade. One teaspoon of turmeric added to the mixture with the mustard is delicious for a change, either when tossing a salad or for marinades.

Vanilla Pod

The vanilla pod is the fruit of a perennial climbing orchid (*Vanilla planifolia*), a native of Central America. The golden

Vanilla Pod

flowers are followed by flat pods six inches in length, which when dried for culinary use are black and shiny like licorice. The perfume is sweet and permeating, and no substitute is considered suitable by connoisseurs, especially in the making of such dishes as French Ice Cream.

A piece of vanilla pod about two inches long should be cut, slit down the centre and used in ice creams, custards, and milk puddings, and infused in the milk for cake mixtures. The piece of pod may be rinsed and used several times. A good place for storing it is in a sugar canister, where it scents the sugar and remains dry and clean. Some people like to keep the vanilla pod in a little cognac, but to my way of thinking the true vanilla flavour is then overpowered. A recipe for producing Vanilla Sugar quickly is given below.

FRENCH ICE CREAM

½ pint milk
½ pint heavy cream
2 inches of vanilla pod
6 egg-yolks
3 oz. sugar

This is a smooth, rich ice cream for special occasions. Split the pod, put it into a saucepan with the milk, scald on a low flame, then stand the pan on one side for 5 minutes or so. Whisk the egg-yolks with the sugar, add to the strained milk, and stir over low heat until thick. Remove from the stove while still stirring. (If it curdles, beat with a rotary beater.) Whip the cream lightly and fold it into the custard. Pour into a chilled refrigerator tray and place in the freezing compartment. Stir once or twice during freezing.

FRENCH ICE CREAM WITH APRICOTS

Make French Ice Cream as in the preceding recipe. Have ready 2 oz. diced glacé apricots which have been soaked in ¼ cup brandy or cognac for at least 2 hours or overnight. Fold into the ice cream before freezing it. A little apricot brandy may be poured over each serving as a sauce.

Vanilla Pod

RICH VANILLA CUSTARD

¾ *pint milk*
yolks of 2 eggs, and
1 *whole egg*

2 *inches of vanilla pod*
2 *scant tablespoons sugar*
1 *dessertspoon butter*

Split the vanilla pod and put it into a saucepan with the milk. Scald the milk, then stand the pan on one side. Beat the eggs with sugar, pour a little of the milk on to them, and return this to the saucepan. Add the butter, and stir over a low flame until thick. Take the pan off the stove and whip the contents with a rotary beater. Pour into a jug and allow to become cool.

QUICK VANILLA SUGAR

If you have an electric blender it takes only a matter of seconds to make this scented sugar for sprinkling on top of custard, whipped cream and stewed fruit, or to dust on biscuits before baking them.

Put 1 cup sugar into a blender, and break half a vanilla pod into pieces and add to the sugar. Blend on high speed until the pod is reduced to black flecks. Keep in a screw-top jar.

Herbal Teas

It would be foolish in a book of this size to try to discuss all the medicinal herbs and their uses. The few that have been mentioned are well known for their health-giving qualities.

A herbal tea, or tisane, is an infusion of boiling water and herbs, either fresh or dried, and is usually taken after dinner or before going to bed, with a little lemon and honey added. They are both pleasant to drink and beneficial, often being a remedy for a mild indisposition. Many people assert that taking them over a long period builds up a resistance to a number of illnesses.

Some well-known herbal teas are those made of lime flowers, orange flowers, lemon-scented verbena leaves, hyssop flowers, bergamot leaves (page 42) and sage leaves (page 139), the last-named herb having once had the reputation of delaying old age. Dried nettle tea is a natural source of iron; rosemary tea is supposed to stimulate the memory; peppermint tea, if taken regularly, helps to ward off colds; mint, lemon-thyme and balm tea in the summer are all refreshing and invigorating, and angelica tea helps digestion.

There are numerous varieties of the camomile daisy growing in many gardens and superficially they look alike, with their finely cut, fern-like leaves and tiny, white-and-gold daisy flower-heads, but there are differences in appearance and their uses are not the same. It is interesting also to note the different botanical headings under which they are known. The most usual kind found in gardens is the old feverfew or febrifuge, *Chrysanthemum parthenium*, and is not used very much today in herbal teas. It was once considered a cure for headaches. Culpeper says with some asperity, 'and if any grumble because they cannot get the herb in winter, tell them, if they please, they may make a syrup of it in summer'.

Both the English camomile (*Anthemis nobilis*), a perennial, and the German camomile (*Matricaria chamomilla*), an annual,

Herbal Teas

are widely used in herbal teas. There seems to be some difference of opinion among herbal writers as to which is the 'true' camomile, and which has the most efficacy. 'Maythen' was the old Saxon name for English camomile, and the Spaniards call it 'manzanilla', meaning little apple. A Spanish wine, flavoured with camomile, is known by the same name; this is also the variety recommended for a camomile lawn. For tea, only the dried flower-heads are used, and these should be gathered early in the morning and spread out to dry on paper in a cool, airy place; when dry put the fragrant heads in clean dry screw-top jars.

German camomile grows to a height of twelve inches and should be planted in a plot by itself and allowed to self-sow as the seed is rather difficult to collect. When the white-and-gold flowers are massed together like this they make a brave show. Harvest and dry the flower-heads in the same way as English camomile. By the way, there is an old saying that where camomile grows the plants in the garden will be healthier.

CAMOMILE TEA (1 CUP)

Measure 1 cup of water into an enamel saucepan and bring to the boil, sprinkle 1 teaspoon of dried camomile heads into the water, put on the lid and boil for $\frac{1}{2}$ minute. Remove from the stove and leave the lid on for a little longer so that the valuable essence is not lost. Strain into a cup, flavour with a little lemon juice and sweeten with honey if you wish. It is delicious.

PEPPERMINT TEA (2 OR 3 CUPS)

The true Mitcham peppermint (*Mentha piperita officinalis*) is used for this tea and is recommended to take as a prevention against colds. The character of this mint's aroma is warmly pungent, while the other mints have a lighter, more piercing quality. Like the rest of the mint family, peppermint prefers a fairly moist position and room to spread. Snails love it so be on guard against these marauders. Tea is made from either fresh or dried leaves: if using fresh leaves, pick a handful from the garden and put them in a crockery teapot, preferably one kept for this purpose, as there is then no taint from ordinary

Herbal Teas

tea present, pour boiling water on to the leaves, cover and leave to infuse for 5 minutes. Sweeten with honey and flavour with lemon. If using the dried leaves, pick a bundle of stalks in the morning after the dew has gone and spread out to dry. When ready strip the leaves from the stems and put in airtight jars. Make the tea in the same way as camomile tea.

MINT TEAS

Dried or fresh mint may be used, and made in the same way as Peppermint Tea.

SPARKLING MINT TEA

(from *The Coronation Cookery Book*, compiled by the Country Women's Association of New South Wales)

3 quarts strong tea
1½ quarts soda water
3 cups castor sugar
¾ pint lemon juice
mint and ice

Make tea in the usual way, allowing 4 teaspoons tea to a quart of boiling water. Infuse and then strain, add sugar, stand it until cool. Stir in lemon juice to tea, add soda and serve in tall glass jug with a lump of ice. Place sprigs of mint on rim of glass and in the jug. A few berries, green grapes or a slice of lemon and orange may be added to each jug. This quantity makes 1¼ gallons, suitable for a large party.

This is a refreshing drink to serve at a tennis party.

NETTLE TEA

Nettle (*Urtica dioica*), the 'wergulu' of early Saxon writings, was with 'maythen', chervil and fennel one of the sacred herbs of those days. It contains iron and protein, and a tisane made of the dried leaves infused in the same way as camomile tea helps a cold. The green beverage has a rich, smooth flavour tasting of all the good green things which come from the earth, and in my opinion is best on its own without lemon and honey.

ROSEMARY TEA

Pick a fresh sprig of rosemary from the garden and put it in a cup, pour boiling water over, stand a saucer on the top to keep

Herbal Teas

in the fumes and leave to infuse for 5 minutes. If making more than 1 cup, pick several sprigs and make the tea in a crockery teapot.

ANGELICA TEA

Pick a few fresh angelica leaves and put them in a crockery teapot; pour boiling water on to them, cover and leave to infuse for 5 minutes.

*

Further recipes will be found on pages 42 (Oswego Tea, with bergamot), 81 (fennel), and 139 (sage).

*

Fragrant Gifts

*

Imagination and willing fingers are the main requirements for making many useful and acceptable gifts which originate from the garden.

Thought and care are important in making the article look attractive. Time is another factor; pot-pourri takes time to mature, pomander balls are a little slow but not difficult to make, and, of course, it is necessary to wait for the lavender to dry before putting it into sachets. A scented gift has the quality of conveying the personality of the giver much more than any other present. A pot-pourri can be a very memorable gift, and one that will stir grateful memories in the receiver. Even during the warmest summer day it will scent a room with fresh perfume, and the hotter the day the more scent it will release. The lid must be replaced at night, and the dried fragrant leaves and flowers stirred frequently.

Fragrant powdered orris root is a necessary ingredient in many of the following recipes and it is interesting to know that it comes from the dried root of the white-flowering Florentine iris, *Iris florentina*. And now for a few gift suggestions.

A POMANDER BALL OR CLOVE ORANGE

It is important to select a ripe, thin-skinned orange. Stick it full of cloves, starting from the stalk-end and going round the orange until it is covered, then roll it well in a teaspoonful of orris powder and a teaspoonful of cinnamon mixed together, pressing the powder well in. Wrap the orange in tissue paper and put it away in a dark cupboard for a week or two. Press a staple into the top of the orange and tie a small bow to it, or thread a yard of narrow ribbon through the staple so that the pomander may hang from a coat-hanger in a wardrobe. Corded ribbon in muted shades of gold, rose, soft blue, lavender or sage green looks particularly attractive with the snuff-brown of the pomander and its old-world appearance.

Fragrant Gifts

A clove orange serves two purposes: it helps to keep moths away from drawers, cupboards and linen closets, as well as scenting them. One hung from the china doorknob of a sitting-room can look charming. The orange becomes 'petrified' and does not decay in any way – it just grows smaller and smaller. Sometimes pomanders ten years old may be seen, still spicily fragrant, as hard as iron, and very, very small.

Here is a delightful poem called 'The Clove Orange' by Eleanor Farjeon:

> *I'll make a clove orange to give to my darling,*
> *I'll make a clove orange to please my delight,*
> *And lay in her coffer to sweeten her linen*
> *And hang by her pillow to sweeten her night.*
>
> *I'll choose a small orange as round as the moon is,*
> *That ripened its cheek in the sunniest grove,*
> *And when it is dry as a midsummer hayfield*
> *I'll stick it all round with the head of a clove.*
>
> *To spice the dull sermon in church of a Sunday,*
> *Her orange of cloves in her bag she shall take;*
> *When parson is prosy and eyelids are drowsy,*
> *One sniff at her spice-ball will charm her awake.*
>
> *And when she walks forth in the highways and byways*
> *Where fevers are prone and infection is rife,*
> *On her palm she shall carry her little clove orange,*
> *A charm against sickness, to guard her sweet life.*
>
> *And moth shall not haunt her most delicate garment,*
> *Nor spectre her delicate dream in the night,*
> *When she hangs in her chamber her little dried orange*
> *I've studded with cloves to delight my Delight.*

LAVENDER BAGS

Pick the lavender heads just before they are in full bloom. Gather them when the dew has gone and before the hot sun has drawn the scent from the blossoms; spread them in a cool airy place to dry, never in direct sunlight because the sun's rays draw out much of the valuable aroma even when picked.

Fragrant Gifts

When dry, rub the tiny flowers from the stalks and fill your lavender bags. If these are not ready, store the dried lavender in an airtight jar. Lavender-coloured muslin or organdie are favourite materials to use for the bags, which are usually drawn in near the top with lavender ribbon tied in a bow. A little silk embroidery enhances the appearance of the sachets. There is scope for the imagination in making lavender bags, and they need not be of the conventional materials and colours – new ideas are always refreshing.

SWEET BAGS

Sweet bags are similar to lavender bags. They are filled with a variety of ingredients, and while lavender bags are used for scenting drawers and linen cupboards, sweet bags may be used not only for this purpose, but for putting under pillows, and hanging on the backs of chairs, where the warmth and pressure from the head releases the perfume. How charmingly thoughtful our grandmothers were, and how unusual and pleasant it would be today for a guest in the spare-room to discover on retiring the fragrance of the sweet bag under her pillow.

The following recipes all are excellent for making sweet bags.

1. Dry equal quantities of lemon-scented geranium and rose-scented geranium leaves. Crumble and mix with the desired amount of dried lavender flowers and a little orris root powder. Fill pastel-coloured silk bags.

2. Take 2 handfuls of dried rose petals, and add 2 oz. of orris root powder, a little common salt, 2 oz. of coriander seeds, 2 teaspoons of cinnamon, 1 teaspoon of ground cloves and 1 handful of dried orange blossom. Mix together and fill sachets.

3. Mix 2 handfuls each of dried wallflowers and rosemary flowers, 2 oz. of orris root powder, and 1 teaspoon of powdered nutmeg. Fill bags. This mixture is particularly aromatic and sweet. The rosemary flowers hold their perfume admirably and mingle well with the warm fragrance of wallflowers.

Fragrant Gifts

A SCENTED COAT-HANGER

Make one of the preparations for a sweet sachet or lavender bag and fill a muslin bag the length of a wooden coat-hanger. Cover the hanger with plain material and sew the filled muslin bag into place on top of the hanger. Cover the hanger completely with a suitable material – silk, sprigged muslin or georgette in pastel colours are all pretty. Softly pleat the material and cover the hook too. An extra touch may be added by swinging a sweet sachet by a length of ribbon from the centre of the hanger.

GIFT PACKAGES

A gift package of home-dried culinary herbs is a welcome present for a friend who is interested in cooking. Cover an old chocolate box or shoe box with pretty wallpaper, preferably one suited to this type of gift, patterned with leaves or flowers, and pack it with small airtight glass jars filled with separate herbs, carefully labelling each one. Paint a leaf or flower on the jar, too, if you wish. A gift package of the tea herbs may be prepared in the same way.

ROSEMARY RUBBING LOTION

Buy 1 pint of odourless rubbing alcohol from the chemist. Put crushed rosemary leaves and flowers, and the highly aromatic seeds, too, if you have them, into a jar. Pour the spirit over, cover and leave for two or three weeks, shaking occasionally. Strain and use. This makes a welcome gift for someone ill in bed. It has a much more pleasant smell than methylated spirit. This recipe may be followed in the same way with other sweet-scented and pungent herbs and flowers, such as lavender, lemon verbena, balm, mint, rose petals, violets, carnations and scented-leaved geraniums.

AROMATICS FOR THE BATH

Sprigs of rosemary are said to be invigorating additions to a bath. A gift package may be made in the way described for culinary herbs. Fill small individual bags of plain coloured muslin with rosemary, pine needles, lavender heads, dried orange flowers and dried eau-de-Cologne mint, naming each herb on the muslin with a marking pencil; these bags are put into a hot bath and allowed to infuse.

SCENTED NOTE-PAPER

Buy a box of white or pastel note-paper and envelopes and slip the sweet-bag mixture in small sachets between the layers of paper and envelopes. Re-wrap the box in cellophane with narrow ribbon finished with a sachet and ribbon-loops on the top. It does not take long for the perfume to permeate the paper.

Here are some old recipes from *The Scented Garden* by E. S. Rohde:

HONEY SOAP

Take four ounces of white soap and as much honey, half an ounce of salt of tartar, and two or three drachms of the distilled Water of fumitory; mix the whole together. This soap cleanses the skin well, and renders it delicately white and smooth. It is also used advantageously to efface the marks of burns and scalds. ('The Toilet of Flora')

SCENTED CANDLES

Take Benjamin, storax, of each foure ounces, Frankincense, Olibanum, of each twelve ounces, Labdanum eighteen ounces, Nigella an ounce, Coriander seeds, Juniper berries, of each halfe an ounce; liquid Storax six ounces, Turpentine halfe an ounce, forme them into Candles with gum: dragant and Rose water. (*The Charitable Physitian*, by Philibert Guibert, Physitian Regent in Paris, 1639)

Some Books Consulted

The Herbarist. A publication of the Herb Society of America. Boston, Massachusetts, 1959.

Harmsworth's Universal Encyclopedia. London (Educational Book Co. Ltd).

Island Recipe Book, compiled by M. O. Blackwell and A. M. Blandy. Vila, New Hebrides, October 1947.

Leyel, Mrs C. F., *The Truth About Herbs.* Culpeper Press, 1954.

Lotions and Potions, compiled by the National Federation of Women's Institutes, 1956. Printed by Novello & Co. Ltd.

Mrs Beeton's Book of Household Management. London (Ward Lock & Co. Ltd), 1906.

Ranson, Florence, *British Herbs.* Harmondsworth (Penguin Books), 1941.

Rohde, Eleanour Sinclair, *Herbs and Herb Gardening.* London (Medici Society), 1936.

Rohde, Eleanour Sinclair, *A Garden of Herbs.* London (Philip Lee Warner, Publisher to the Medici Society Ltd). Also Boston, U.S.A.

Thompson, Flora, *Lark Rise to Candleford.* London (Reprint Society), 1948.

Webster, Helen Noyes, *Herbs: How to Grow Them and How to Use Them.* Boston (Charles T. Branford Company), revised and enlarged edition 1947.

White, Florence, *Good English Food (Local and Regional).* London (Jonathan Cape), 1952.

Herb Stockists

ARMY & NAVY STORES LTD, 105 Victoria Street, London SW1, 01-834 1234.

THE BOMBAY EMPORIUM, Radiant House, Pegamoid Road, Edmonton N18 2NG: full range of spices, some herbs and all curry ingredients.

CAMISA & SON, 61 Old Compton Street, London W1, 01-437 7610.

CHILTERN HERB FARMS LTD, Buckland Common, Tring, Hertfordshire: dried herbs, herbal teas and other herbal products.

COUNTRY STYLE, Ship Street, Brighton, Sussex: full range of English and continental herbs and spices.

E. & A. EVETTS, Ashfields Herb Nursery, Hinstock, Market Drayton, Shropshire.

FORTNUM & MASON LTD, 181 Piccadilly, London W1, 01-734 8040.

HARRODS LTD, Knightsbridge, London SW1, 01-730 1234.

HEATH & HEATHER LTD, Ridgmont Road, St Albans, Hertfordshire.

HELLENIC PROVISION STORES, 25 Charlotte Street, London W1, 01-636 4406: full range of herbs used in Greek cookery.

HERB FARM LTD, Seal, Sevenoaks, Kent: fresh herbs for planting, dried herbs and other herbal products.

JACKSONS OF PICCADILLY, 171 Piccadilly, London W1, 01-493 1033.

LOUIS ROCHE LTD, 14 Old Compton Street, London W1, 01-437 4588: fresh French herbs, including some for planting, and selected spices.

SELFRIDGES LTD, Oxford Street, London W1, 01-629 1234.

WHOLEFOOD, 112 Baker Street, London W1, 01-935 3924.

HERB SEEDS AND PLANTS

BUNYARDS, Maidstone, Kent.
THE HERB FARM, Seal, Sevenoaks, Kent.
THE HERB FARM, Stoke Lacey, Herefordshire.
JOHN JEFFERIES, Cirencester, Gloucestershire.
SUTTONS, Reading, Berkshire.
THOMPSON MORGAN, Ipswich, Suffolk.

Index

accompaniments with curry, 71ff.
ale, mulled, 31
Alexandra's fruit and poppy-seed pudding, 122
allspice, 25
angelica, 27; candied, 27
angelica leaves and rhubarb, stewed, 28
angelica tea, 166
aniseed (anise), 29
aniseed carrots, 30
aniseed cookies, 30
apple, baked, with geranium leaves, 87
apple and bergamot with pork sausages, 41
apple crumble with coriander, 68
apple juice with veal, 101
apple pudding, 66
apricots with French ice cream, 159
Arabian stuffed capsicums, 67
aspic: basil and tomato, 35; cabbage, 50
aromatic bath, 94
aromatics for the bath, 172
aromatic sweet potatoes, 51
attar-of-roses sponge, 85
aubergine and tahina appetizer, 146
avocado and chervil, iced, 53
avocado and crab mould, 149
avocado Mexican guacamole, 57
avocado soup, 97

baby marrows, buttered, 155
baked fish with cider, 142
baked tomatoes with basil, 34
balm, 31
balm and marshmallow custard, 32
balm and orange frosted (drink), 32

balm dressing with orange salad, 32
bananas, flaming, 62
bananas with veal chops, 67
barbecue baked beans, 56
basil, 33; baked tomatoes with, 34
basil and tomato aspic, 35
basil vinegar, 34
bath, aromatic, 94; cosmetic, 44
bay leaves, 37
beans: barbecue baked, 56; haricot, and lamb, 117; haricot, sweet-sour, 61; haricot, with tomatoes, 53
beef, in Welsh stew, 38
beef and tomatoes, 125
beef casserole, with bay leaves and walnuts, 38
beef casserole with rosemary, 125
beef teriyaki, 88
beet bortsch, 64
beetroot and cardomom salad, 47
bergamot, 40
bergamot salad, 41
bergamot sauce, 42
bird's-eye pepper, 56
borage, 42
bortsch, 64
bouillabaisse, 133
bouquet garni, 37, 98
brawn, with bergamot salad, 41
bread, sage, 138
buns, saffron, 133
burning steak, 101
butter, herb, 118
butter, with aniseed, etc., for hot rolls, 29

buttered baby marrows, 155
buttered cabbage spines, 126

181

Index

cabbage, red, casserole with pork sausages, 29
cabbage aspic, 50
cabbage leaves, stuffed, 38
cabbage salad with dill, 76
cabbage spines, buttered, 126
cake: attar-of-roses sponge, 85; Christmas, 62; coriander honey, 68; poppy-seed, 122; spiced tea, 68
camomile, 163
camomile lawn, 18
camomile tea, 164
candied angelica, 27
candied rose petals, 128
candles, scented, 173
capsicums, 48; Arabian stuffed, 67
caramel custard, 43
caraway rice ring and tuna fish, 45
caraway seed, 44
cardamom and baked pears, 47
cardamom and beetroot salad, 47
cardamom honey dressing, 48
cardamom seed, 46
carnation petals, crystallized, 43
carrots, aniseed, 30
casserole of beef, 125
casserole sausages with cider, 82
cayenne, 48
celery seed, 50
cheese, cream, with chives, 58
cheese and mint dressing, 105
cheese and pineapple in the shell, 45
cheese and sage omelette, 137
cheese spread with dill, 77
cheese spread with sage, 135
cheese straws, 49
chervil, 51
chervil and avocado, 53
chicken curry, 73
chicken juniper, 91
chicken livers in wine, 148
chicken mimosa, 150
chicken mould, 155
chicken suprême with peaches, 148
chicken teriyaki, 88
chicory, 54
chicory and eggs, 55
chicory salad, 55
chilli con carne, 57
chilli pepper, 48
chilli powder, 56
chives, 58
chops, veal, with coriander, 67
Christmas cake, 62
chutney, lemon and mustard seed, 108
cider with baked fish, 142
cider with casserole sausages, 82
cinnamon, 59
clove orange, 63, 169
cloves, 63
coat-hanger, scented, 172
coconut milk, 73
cole slaw with dill, 76
continental poppy-seed cake, 122
cookies, anise, 30; oatmeal and sesame, 146
coriander and honey cakes, 68
coriander apple crumble, 68
coriander seed, 66
cosmetic bath, 44
cottage pie, 99
courgettes, buttered, 155
crab and avocado mould, 149
crab paprika, 115
creamed cucumber, 58
creams, rose, 26
cress, 107
crystallized flowers, 43
crystallized mint leaves, 106
cucumber: creamed, 58; Turkish, 70
cucumber in dill pickles, 75
cudweed, 147
cultivation of herbs, 14ff. *See also* individual herbs
cumin and rose-geranium drops, 70
cumin seed, 69
curry: chicken, 73; Indian, 71; Indonesian, 73; meat, 72

Index

curry powder, 71
custard: balm and marshmallow, 32; caramel, 43; lemon-scented, 86; mint and marshmallow, 105; vanilla, 159

damask roses, 127
Devonshire junket, 62
dill-cheese dip, 77
dill pickles, 75
dill sauce, 77
dill seed, 74
dill with cole slaw, 76
dill with scallops, 76
dolmas, 36
dough, 111
dressing: balm, 32; cardamom honey, 48; French: with basil, 34, with bergamot, 41, with turmeric, 158; mint and cheese, 105
dried herbs, 18ff.
drying, 18ff.
dumplings, sunny saffron, 132; tomato, 49

eau-de-Cologne mint, *see* mint
egg and potato pie, 49
egg tart, minted, 104
eggs and chicory, 55
Emily's pastry, 136
English lavender, 94

fennel, 78; cooked, 79
fennel cream sauce, 79
fennel potato cake, 81
fennel tea, 81
festive ham, 65
finocchio, *see* fennel
fish: baked, with cider, 142; savory stuffing for, 143
fish kedgeree, 157
fish meunière, 108
fish pie with herbs, 59
fish roe entrée, 36
fish special, 39
fish suprême, 96
flaming bananas, 62
French dressing, *see* dressing
French ice cream, 159; with apricots, 159
French lavender, 94
French omelette with chives, 59
French-style peas, 105
fried orange slices, 26
fried parsley, 118
fried tripe with savory, 141
fruit and poppy-seed pudding, 122

garlic, 81
geranium, 83; apple, with baked apples, 87; lemon, custard, 86; peppermint, jelly, 86; rose, and cumin drops, 70; jelly, 26; sponge, 85
gift packages, 172
ginger, 87
glazed pears, 28
gooseberry shortcake, saffron, 134
goulash, Hungarian veal, 114
grape juice and savory jelly, 143
green butter, 118
green ginger, 87
growing herbs, 14ff. *See also* individual herbs
Gruyère with veal, 92
guacamole, Mexican, 57

hair rinse, rosemary, 127
hair tonic, sage, 138
halva, 145
ham, festive, 65
ham and sweet potato pie, 109
haricot beans, sweet-sour, 61
haricot beans and lamb, 117
haricot beans with tomatoes, 53
harvesting herbs, 19ff.
herb butter, 118
herb gardens, 14ff.
herb lawns, 17ff.
herb scones, 101
honey and cardamom dressing, 48

Index

honey and coriander cake, 68
honey of roses, 129
honey soap, 173
hot slaw, 77
Hungarian veal goulash, 114

ice, parsley, 118
ice cream: French, 159; with apricots, 159
Indian curry, 71
Indian mint sauce, 71
Indonesian curry, 73
indoor herb-growing, 20ff.
Isabelle's sage and cheese omelette, 137

jam, rose-petal, 128
Jamaica pepper, *see* allspice
jelly: mint, 106; parsley, 117; peppermint, 86; rose-geranium, 26; savory and grape juice, 143
juniper, chicken, 91
juniper berries, 90
juniper sauerkraut, 91
junket, Devonshire, 62

kebabs, 110
kedgeree, 157
Kheer, 46
kidneys and mushrooms with fennel, 80
kümmel, 44

ladder-garden, 14
lamb, savory-stuffed, 142
lamb haricot, 117
lamb shanks Armenian, 70
lamb's liver in dolmas, 36
lamb's liver with basil, 35
lavender, 92
lavender bags, 170
lavender cotton, 95
lavender sugar, 94
lavender vinegar, 94
lavender water, 94
lawn, herb, 17

leek tart with sage, 136
lemon and mustard seed chutney, 108
lemon balm, 31
lemon-scented baked custard, 86
lemon thyme, *see* thyme
lentils and sausages, 120
liver, lamb's: with basil, 35; in dolmas, 36
livers, chicken, in wine, 148

mace, 95
mango mousse, 89
marjoram, 98
marjoram scones, 101
marjoram vinegar, 102
marmalade with coriander, 69
marshmallow and balm custard, 32
marshmallow and mint custard, 105
mayonnaise, sharp (with celery seed), 51
meat balls in sauce, 155
meat loaf, 154
Mexican guacamole, 57
milk, rabbit cooked in, 154
mint, 102
mint and cheese dressing, 105
mint and marshmallow custard, 105
mint jelly, 106
mint julep, 106
mint leaves, crystallized, 43, 106
mint sauce, 104; Indian, 71
mint teas, 165
minted egg tart, 104
mousse, mango or peach, 89
mugwort, 147
mulled ale, 31
mushrooms and kidneys with fennel, 80
mushrooms and noodles, 117
mustard seed, 107
mustard seed and lemon chutney, 108

184

Index

nettle tea, 165
Newburg sauce, 48
noodles, poppy-seed, 121
noodles and mushrooms, 117
nutmeg, 95

oatmeal and sesame cookies, 146
olives oregano, 112
omelette: with chives, 59; sage, with cheese, 137
onions: pickled, 120; and sage stuffing, 137; studded with cloves, in cooking, 63
orange, clove, 169
orange and balm frosted (drink), 32
orange salad with balm dressing, 32
orange slices, fried, 26
oregano, 109
orris root powder, 130
Oswego tea (bergamot), 42
oysters Bercy, 99
oysters in savory fish stuffing, 143

paprika, 113; crab, 115
parsley, 115; fried, 118
parsley butter, 118
parsley ice, 118
parsley jelly, 117
pastry, short, Emily's, 136; rich, 100; vatroushki recipe, 64
peach mousse, 89
peaches with chicken suprême, 148
pears: baked, and cardamom, 47; glazed, 28
peas, French-style, 105
pennyroyal lawn, 17. *See also* mint
pepper, 119
pepper, Jamaica, *see* allspice
peppercorns, 119
peppermint jelly, 186
peppermint tea, 164
pickled onions, 120
pickles, dill, 75
pie: cottage, or shepherd's, 99; fish, with herbs, 59; pizza, 110; potato, 100; potato and egg, 49; ham and sweet potato, 109
pimento, *see* allspice
pineapple, with festive ham, 65
pineapple and cheese in the shell, 45
pineapple cocktail, 107
pizza pie, 110
pomander ball, 169
poppy seed, 120
poppy seed cake, 122
poppy seed noodles, 121
poppy seed pudding, Alexandra's, 122
pork teriyaki, 88
potato and egg pie, 49
potato cake, fennel-seed, 81
potato pie, 100
potato salad, tropical, 158
potato soup, 52
potatoes, *see also* sweet potatoes
pot-pourri, 129
poultry, thyme stuffing for, 156

quiche Lorraine, 113
quick vanilla sugar, 160

rabbit cooked in milk, 154
rarebit: savoury Welsh, 97; Welsh with sage, 137
red cabbage casserole with pork sausages, 29
relish, red tomato, 89
rhubarb and angelica leaves, stewed, 28
rice and treacle pudding, 39
rice ring, caraway, with tuna fish, 45
rice salad with herbs, 34
rich vanilla custard, 159
risotto, saffron, 132
roe, fish, entrée, 36
rosebuds, crystallized, 43
rose creams, 26
rose-geranium and cumin drops, 70
rose-geranium jelly, 26

Index

rosemary, 123
rosemary hair rinse, 127
rosemary rubbing lotion, 172
rosemary scones, 126
rosemary snow, 126
rosemary tea, 165
rose-petal jam, 128
rose petals: candied, 128; with green salad, 128
rose vinegar, 128
rose water, 130
roses, 127
rubbing lotion, rosemary, 172
rum toddy, 60

saffron, 131
saffron buns, 133
saffron dumplings, 132
saffron gooseberry shortcake, 134
saffron risotto, 132
sage, 134
sage and cheese omelette, 137
sage and cheese spread, 135
sage and onion stuffing, 137
sage bread, 138
sage hair tonic, 138
sage in leek tart, 136
sage tea, 139
sage with Welsh rarebit, 137
salad: beetroot and cardamom, 47; bergamot, with brawn, 41; chicory, 55; green, with rose petals, 128; orange, with balm dressing, 32; rice, with herbs, 34; seafood, 53; sesame seed, 145; tropical potato, 158; Waldorf, 114
salt, 139; seasoned, 140
sandwiches, 14n., 98, 104
sauce: bergamot, 42; dill, 77; fennel cream, 79; hollandaise, 149; Indian mint, 71; mint, 104; Newburg, 48; savory tomato, 143; suprême, 150; tartare, 149
sauerkraut, juniper, 91
sausage, fennel seed, 80
sausage casserole with cider, 82

sausages and lentils, 120
sausages with apple and bergamot, 41
sausages with red cabbage casserole, 29
savory, 140
savory and grape juice jelly, 143
savory-stuffed lamb, 142
savory stuffing (for fish), 143
savory tomato sauce, 143
savory with fried tripe, 141
savoury meat balls, 155
savoury meat loaf, 154
savoury Welsh rarebit, 97
scallops with dill, 76
scented candles, 173
scented coat-hanger, 172
scented-leaved geraniums, 83. *See also* geraniums
scented note-paper, 173
scones: herb, 101; rosemary, 126
seafood salad, 53
seed cake, 46
sesame and oatmeal cookies, 145
sesame seed, 144
sesame-seed salad, 145
sharp mayonnaise, 51
shortcake, saffron gooseberry, 134
short pastry: Emily's, 136; rich, 100; vatroushki recipe, 64
slaw: cole, 76; hot, 77
smallage, 50
snow, rosemary, 126
soup: avocado, 97; potato, 52; spinach, 53; southernwood, 147
spaghetti bolognese, 112
spearmint, 102
spiced tea cake, 68
spiced veal roll, 25
spiced vinegar, 120
spinach soup, 53
sponge cake: attar-of-roses, 85; seed, 46
steak, burning, 101
steak casserole with bay leaves and pickled walnuts, 38

Index

steak kebabs, 110
steak rolls, stuffed, 83
steak with oregano, 110
stew, Welsh, 38
stuffed cabbage leaves, 38
stuffed capsicums, Arabian, 67
stuffed steak rolls, 83
stuffing: with juniper berries, 90; sage and onion, 137; savory, for fish, 143; thyme, for poultry, 156; turkey, 156
succory, 54
sugar: lavender, 94; vanilla, 159, 160
summer savory, *see* savory
sunny saffron dumplings, 132
suprême sauce, 150
sweet potato and ham pie, 109
sweet potatoes, 51
sweet-sour haricot beans, 61

tahina, 144
tahina and aubergine appetizer, 146
tarragon, 146
tarragon vinegar, 151
tartare sauce, 149
tea: angelica, 166; bergamot, 42; camomile, 164; fennel, 81; mint, 165; nettle, 165; Oswego, 42; peppermint, 164; rosemary, 165; sage, 139
tea cake, spiced, 68
teeth, whiten with sage, 139
ten-minute crab paprika, 115
teriyaki, meat, 88
thyme, 151
thyme lawn, 17, 153
thyme stuffing for poultry, 156
Tia Maria, with baked pears, 47
tisane, 163
toddy, rum, 60
tomato and basil aspic, 35
tomato dumplings, 49

tomato relish, red, 89
tomato sauce with savory, 143
tomatoes, baked, with basil, 35
tomatoes and beef, 125
tomatoes with haricot beans, 53
treacle and rice pudding, 39
treacle tart, 61
tripe, fried, with savory, 141
tropical potato salad, 158
tuna fish with caraway rice ring, 45
turkey stuffing, 156
Turkish cucumbers, 70
turmeric, 157

vanilla custard, 159
vanilla pod, 158
vanilla sugar, quick, 160
vatroushki, 64
veal chops, baked (with coriander), 67
veal goulash, Hungarian, 114
veal Gruyère, 92
veal roll, spiced, 25
veal teriyaki, 88
veal with apple juice, 101
vegetable tart, 100
vinegar: basil, 34; lavender, 94; marjoram, 102; rose, 128; spiced, 120; tarragon, 151
violets, crystallized, 43

Waldorf salad, 114
wallflowers, 17
walnuts, pickled, in steak casserole, 38
Welsh rarebit, 97; with sage, 137
Welsh stew, 38
wheel-garden, 14
winter savory, *see* savory
wormwood, 147

zucchini, buttered, 156

MORE ABOUT PENGUINS AND PELICANS

Penguinews, which appears every month, contains details of all the new books issued by Penguins as they are published. From time to time it is supplemented by *Penguins in Print*, which is a complete list of all titles available. (There are some five thousand of these.)

A specimen copy of *Penguinews* will be sent to you free on request. For a year's issues (including the complete lists) please send 50p if you live in the British Isles, or 75p if you live elsewhere. Just write to Dept EP, Penguin Books Ltd, Harmondsworth, Middlesex, enclosing a cheque or postal order, and your name will be added to the mailing list.

In the U.S.A.: For a complete list of books available from Penguin in the United States write to Dept CS, Penguin Books Inc., 7110 Ambassador Road, Baltimore, Maryland 21207.

In Canada: For a complete list of books available from Penguin in Canada write to Penguin Books Canada Ltd, 41 Steelcase Road West, Markham, Ontario.

Elizabeth David

ENGLISH COOKING, ANCIENT AND MODERN
Spices, Salt and Aromatics in the English Kitchen

In this volume, the first in an original study of English cooking, Elizabeth David presents English recipes which are notable for their employment of spices, salt and aromatics. As usual, she seasons instruction with information, explaining the origins and uses of such ingredients as nutmeg, cardamom and juniper. Mrs David stresses the influence of centuries of oriental trade on the English kitchen, where spices and Indian curry, kebabs and yoghurt are now perfectly at home, along with immigrant dishes such as risotto, paella and pepper steak.

This book, with its brawns (or pig's-head cheese), briskets and spiced beef, its smoked fish and cured pork, its old-fashioned curd dishes and sweet fruit pickles, sounds a welcome, if uncommon, note in the English kitchen.

Elizabeth David

'She has the happy knack of giving just as much detail as the average cook finds desirable; she presumes neither on our knowledge nor on our ignorance' – Elizabeth Nicholas in the *Sunday Times*

MEDITERRANEAN FOOD

A practical collection of recipes made by the author when she lived in France, Italy, the Greek Islands and Egypt, evoking all the colour of the Mediterranean but making use of ingredients obtainable in England.

FRENCH COUNTRY COOKING

Some of the splendid regional variations in French cookery are described in this book.

FRENCH PROVINCIAL COOKING

'It is difficult to think of any home that can do without Elizabeth David's *French Provincial Cooking* ... One could cook for a lifetime on the book alone' – *Observer*

ITALIAN FOOD

Exploding once and for all the myth that Italians live entirely on minestrone, spaghetti and veal escalopes, this exciting book demonstrates the enormous and colourful variety of Italy's regional cooking.

SUMMER COOKING

A selection of summer dishes that are light (not necessarily cold), easy to prepare and based on the food in season.